PREY

Books by
CARL RICHARDS

SELECTIVE TROUT

FLY-FISHING STRATEGY

EMERGERS

BACKCOUNTRY FLY FISHING IN SALT WATER:
An Innovative Guide to Some of the Finest
and Most Interesting Fishing in Salt Water

(*all the above with Doug Swisher*)

STONEFLIES (*with Fred Arbona*)

PREY

PREY

Carl Richards

Illustrated by Mike Gouse

*Pattern photography
by Bob Braendle*

THE LYONS PRESS
Guilford, Connecticut

An imprint of The Globe Pequot Press

The Lyons Press is an imprint of The Globe Pequot Press.

Originally published in hardcover by The Lyons Press, 1995

Printed in the United States

10 9 8 7 6 5 4 3 2 1

The Library of Congress Cataloging-in-Publication Data is available on file.

ISBN 1-58574-541-3

Contents

Acknowledgments

A number of people helped me with this book, and I would like to thank them for their work.

First of all, my thanks to Nick Lyons, my editor and publisher, who made the book possible.

My wife Alecia, for editorial assistance and for putting up with my frequent disappearances to the salt.

Robert Braendle, who did the black-and-white photography and the color of the artificials for the book, along with assisting me in collecting some of the prey, and for being a good fishing companion.

My thanks to Captain Doug Swisher and Captain Bob Marvin for introducing me to the backcountry.

George Germain for help with collecting specimens, keeping the boat running, and being my fishing friend.

Allen Fici, who helped me collect prey.

To Tim Fox and Jerry Klavins, besides being good friends, my thanks for making it possible to fish the Golden Bonefish Lodge and collect many creatures that have never been photographed.

Arthur C. Costonis introduced me to the Myaka River Pass and photographed the scaled sardine for me.

Thanks to Jim Bloom and Jim Ostead, who assisted me in collecting in the Bahamas.

Dr. David K. Camp, Dr. Richard Matheson, Mr. Peter Hood and Mr. David Pierce, of the Florida Marine Research Institute, who very graciously helped me in identifying prey species.

Bruce Willson and Larry Woods, who made the boat possible.

Introduction

During the last few years I have spent a considerable amount of time studying saltwater-bait naturals and their imitations. I have done this because I feel a need, for me at least, to fish with flies that simulate what gamefish really eat. I find the research fascinating, and creating new patterns is fun. The only pursuit more enjoyable is catching fish on a newly designed pattern. Most experienced anglers agree that they have often wished for better patterns when fish are in a frenzy and feeding on a specific bait form. This is especially true during periods when large numbers of one prey species are swarming. In my experience, all gamefish become very selective under these conditions. The most accurate imitations are almost always the most productive.

Feeding frenzy of snook under dock lights.

For hundreds of years, intense study has gone into insect imitations. Mayflies, caddis and stoneflies have been exhaustively examined and copied. Comparatively little work has gone into freshwater prey such as forage fish and crayfish. Relatively speaking, almost no effective work has been done to study saltwater prey species. The huge number of different saltwater baits is mind-boggling. Many angler/entomologists know the exact number of mayflies on the North American continent and can even give you their Latin names. No one knows the number of shrimp species living along the Atlantic, Pacific, and Gulf coasts. Very few anglers would even recognize a mantis shrimp. This is a large area of fly imitation that has barely been touched. It needs, and will undoubtedly receive, more study with the increasing interest in saltwater angling. This book will stress saltwater patterns, but it will include freshwater patterns such as minnows, young fish, and crayfish that lend themselves to the same tying techniques as saltwater-bait forms.

CHAPTER ONE

Characteristics of a Successful Pattern

I have two main goals when designing imitations. If they are achieved, the results will be patterns that are realistic in appearance, fish well, and catch fish during the most selective situations. My first goal is to produce a fly as close in appearance as possible to an important food source that induces feeding frenzies in gamefish. I will go to almost any length to achieve as exact an imitation as possible. Later, I will attempt to simplify the pattern. My second goal is to design a fly that fishes well. If the pattern cannot be made to act like the natural, it will not catch fish. If it can't be manipulated to swim, dive, or crawl like its live counterpart, it will not be a successful pattern.

There are six factors I feel should be incorporated into a good design. All are important, but some are more important than others. The following are six factors in their order of importance to me.

Sardine imitation coming through water with a jack after it.

1

1. The pattern must appear alive and feel alive in the water. It should have a natural lifelike action and feel natural to the mouth of a gamefish on the strike. A baitfish imitation should be tied with materials that undulate when retrieved, or even when no movement is imparted except by the current. A superrealistic-looking fly dressed with stiff, hard materials will not be very effective, as any nymph fisherman can attest.

2. The pattern must be able to be manipulated in such a way as to mimic the swimming, crawling, or diving action of the natural. The fly, when retrieved, must be designed so it can be made to react as prey reacts to gamefish when attacked. An example of this would be a crustacean such as a snapping shrimp. These creatures do not possess genius I.Q., but they are clever enough to realize they cannot outswim a bonefish. They face their attacker and use their natural camouflage to attempt to sneak away when they believe they are unobserved. Thus a snapping shrimp imitation must be designed so it will mimic this characteristic of the natural as the fly line is stripped back.

Hair shrimpy coming through water with a snook after it.

3. The pattern should be soft or at least resilient. It should not be rock-hard because fish quickly reject hard objects. Even bottom feeders such as redfish, which can crush clams and crabs, prefer the soft-shelled phase, just as smallmouth bass prefer soft-shelled crayfish over hard-shelled crayfish.

4. The pattern should be as easy to cast as possible. It should be light in weight and have the least air resistance that can be incorporated into the shape. Light weight and low air resistance would be the ideal, although with some shapes like crabs the ideal is not always possible. Even so, an unwieldy shape can be designed to improve and lighten the fly.

5. The pattern should be nonfouling when cast. This attribute can be difficult to achieve when designing certain baitfish imitations that have odd shapes. This is especially true when the dressing for the fly includes the most lifelike undulating materials. I do the best I can, but I will accept some fouling if it is offset by a very lifelike pattern.

A fouled streamer with tail around hook.

6. The pattern should be durable. A perfect tie would never disintegrate even after being mauled by one hundred tarpon. This degree of durability is of course unrealistic since some of the most lifelike materials are the least durable. I will always pick realism over durability. Since I tie my own flies, durability is not so important, but if you are producing flies to sell, it would probably save you some disgruntled customers to substitute sturdier materials.

A barracuda's mouth destroying a fly.

CHAPTER TWO

A Systematic Method of Designing Realistic Prey Imitations

The tyer cannot design a realistic imitation unless he knows what he wants to imitate and exactly what the natural looks like. He must first learn what his target fish eat in order to find out what he needs to imitate. With trout or smallmouth bass, this is easy because so much study has gone into the subject. With snook, redfish, and most other saltwater gamefish this is not so easy because comparatively little research has been done. So for salt gamefish I ask baitfishermen, local guides, and the owners of local bait shops. These people know what is going on in the area. They usually catch their own bait and they know and use the bait that works. Most are more than willing to share any knowledge they possess and are generally friendly and helpful. I then collect specimens of small fish and invertebrates in the area in which I will be fishing. This tells me what is available at the time.

Once I decide on the food form to imitate, I then must discover exactly what it looks like. I'll use a Spanish sardine as an example (see color photograph section), for this is one of the favorite prey of most saltwater gamefish. In addition, it is a member of the herring family, of which there are many species found in both fresh- and saltwater, and almost all have the same general shape and coloration. All are prime food forms, and if I can create an effective pattern for Spanish sardines, I then, with a little modification, will have an effective pattern for the entire herring family.

An absolute must in this process is to get a good macrophotograph of the natural I want to imitate. With it I will see all the details and colors that are there and I won't be relying on faulty memory or false impressions. Although it is much better to take your own photographs, color plates are available for most species in the various field guides. These are listed in the bibliography and are a good way to get started.

Collection

After I have decided what prey to imitate, I need to collect live specimens and take macrophotos of them immediately in the field. Several tools are employed when capturing specimens. One of the best is a cast net that will take any bait in the area except very slim minnows. This type of net is ideal for Spanish sardines and it will also take shrimp, crabs and other baitfish.

A simple dip net is useful at night under lights where bait is attracted to the area by the illumination. These are best for very small fish that will slip through the larger weave of a cast net. They are perfect when collecting the phototropic anchovies and glass minnows usually found swarming under lighted bridges when the tide is moving. Blue crabs and other swimming crabs can also be caught with a dip net along shallow bars and flats.

At low tide when flats are exposed, a shovel and a coffee tin with one end open can be used to capture the many creatures burrowing in the substratum. These will include marine worms, crabs, snapping shrimp, mantis and shore shrimp. Again at low tide, crab species such as mangrove and mud crabs can be collected by picking through oyster-shell clumps found at the base of mangrove trees and along oyster bars. Fiddler crabs can be handpicked on many beaches in the intertidal zone. Seines can be used along shorelines and will get everything but the burrowers. Many baitfish can be caught with a small gold hook, and line minnow traps, purchased at tackle stores, can be baited with crackers or cat food and left to fish for themselves.

A new product called a "Yabby Pump" is now available to gather burrowing forms like marine worms, crabs, and shrimp. It is manufactured in Australia and resembles a bicycle pump. A hose is inserted into a hole in sand or mud, and the animal trapped in it is sucked out onto a screen. The pumps can be ordered from Standard Bait Pumps, Alvery Reels, Z6 Antinomy St. Carole Park Q.L.D. 4300 Australia.

Author using a cast net.

Author using a dip net.

Author collecting mud crabs at low tide on a mangrove-lined bay with oyster bars around the shoreline.

Seine on a shoreline.

Photography

Once the specimen has been collected, I attempt to get pictures immediately while the organism is still alive. This is critical because most baitfish, and many invertebrates, lose color rapidly when stressed let alone when they're dead. This is especially true of sardines, which are notoriously fragile. Crabs change more slowly and are much easier to keep alive and they may be transported to the home base and chilled for ease of staging the picture.

The camera I most frequently use is an Olympus OM2N single-lens reflex with a 50mm "macro" lens. If I need more magnification than this lens alone will give me, I add a 2X teleconverter or a bellows. The OM2N has an automatic and a manual setting and is quite versatile. I like this camera because it is smaller and lighter than most single-lens reflex cameras, so I am not reluctant to carry it on the stream. Newer versions like the OM4N have improvements including better light meters and bodies built of titanium for more durability. The strobe I use with the OM2N is an OM System Electronic Flash T32 with a power bounce grip. The tripod I prefer is a Cullman Miniature. It is durable and compact and easy to carry in the field. I have recently acquired an Olympus IS3 DLX camera, which is a single-lens reflex without the need to change lenses. This is a state-of-the-art, computerized model with fuzzy logic. This camera makes it very easy to get excellent pictures without a lot of setup time. It's almost impossible to take a bad picture with it. The IS3 DLX has a 35mm to 180mm autofocusing zoom lens, with 28mm wide-angle, 300mm tele-photo, and macro screw-in lenses as additions. The camera carries a built-in high-power dual-strobe "intelligent" flash, which allows shots of natural prey at night and in bad light. This is very important in the field because many subjects must be photographed within minutes of capture or much of the color is lost.

The film I use is Ektrachrome Elite. Some publishers tell me they prefer Fujicrome because they feel it gives more intense color, but for my own use I do not want more than is actually there. I usually shoot ASA 400 in the field. It is a little more grainy than the lower numbers, but I am not going to enlarge much, and the Elite reproduces every detail if you don't try to enlarge it too much. The ASA 400 allows me to close down the f-stop to f-22 so I can get as much depth of field as possible. It is not practical to shoot a very slow, fine-grained film (such as ASA 25) if most of the subject is out of focus. After I have taken the slides, I want some of the best made into prints to keep at the tying desk for reference. This is less trouble than carrying two cameras and shooting both print and slide film. I need slides for shows, books, and articles—publishers want transparencies for reproduction—but if I am only going to use the pictures for tying, I will shoot Kodak Gold print film.

Camera and aquarium—Olympus Is-3.

My normal setup for pictures of live fish, shrimp, and other bait forms is as follows: a small aquarium is filled with water and placed on a stand. The camera is attached to the tripod and placed in front of the aquarium, and a neutral, nonreflective background is positioned behind it. The neutral background is used so the light meter is not thrown off and the pictures are correctly exposed. If I am using the strobe, I have the camera slightly above the subject I have placed in the aquarium, so the light strikes the glass at a 45° angle. This eliminates glare on the film. If I am not using the strobe, this step is not necessary. I always bracket the shot, by taking exposures two f-stops on either side of the one I think is correct. In general, very dark subjects require more light and very light subjects need less light.

Fragile subjects such as glass minnows and sardines must be photographed immediately or they lose most of their color; glass minnows will even disintegrate. Crabs and hardier fish like mullet should be kept alive and may be shot at leisure.

There are problems in photographing small baitfish. This is because all fish, and especially smaller forage species, reflect different colors, depending on the angle light rays strike the body. This means the camera will produce pictures that can vary greatly in color. If a baitfish is held in the palm of the hand and slowly rotated, the human eye will also record these different colors. The colors will also change when the fish is photographed at varying depths of water. This is because water absorbs some colors sooner than other colors. One example of this phenomenon is that in six feet of water the color red looks green. Making this photography even more difficult is the fact that some baitfish appear much different at night when a light is shined on them. Here again, different angles of light will produce varying colors.

The most striking examples of these phenomena I know of are certain members of the herring family, especially scaled sardines and thread herring. When a light is shined on these species at night the neural column fluoresces a vivid green and the sides are iridescent with every color in the rainbow. In daylight, these dramatic colors are greatly reduced.

My solutions to these problems are to get shots at varying angles, both in and out of the water, at night and in daylight. Then in designing a pattern I try to incorporate all the colors I have seen in the field and recorded in the pictures into the fly. I hope the materials will change color at different depths as the natural does. This is by no means a perfect solution, but the method seems to be practical because the patterns catch fish, even under the most selective situations.

Designing the Pattern

With good color prints at hand, I am now prepared to begin designing the pattern. First I draw a picture of the natural, noting mentally unusual colors and features. While I am making the drawing, I envision how I can imitate the shape with various tying materials. After completing the drawing, I sketch a hook and begin drawing fly-tying materials on the hook in the order I would tie them on if dressing the actual fly. While I am doing this, I am considering what materials will produce the most lifelike action and be true to the criteria for a successful pattern as explained in Chapter 1.

In order to be able to choose the best materials, the tyer must be completely familiar with what is available. Some of the most interesting fly-tying materials are not found in fly shops or tying catalogues. I have discovered marvelous fly makings in hobby shops, craft stores, and weaver shops. When I began developing a realistic sardine, the best material for the deep belly was either pure-white silk brick or a 50/50 mix of silk and lambs' wool. I discovered these materials in a weaver shop and, as far as I know, they are not available anywhere else. The eyes come from a lure material company. They are the most realistic eyes I have ever seen. When five-minute epoxy is placed over them, they have a three-dimensional quality. A full list of materials I use, their good and bad properties, and where to obtain the more unusual ones, will be discussed in the next chapter.

Testing

The last step is at least as important as the others. Once I have completed a pattern, I test it by taking it fishing. The fly must perform in the water as I'd envisioned it performing when I designed it. I once crafted a beautiful baitfish imitation that looked great in the water. But it had one fatal flaw—it swam upside down. This is not an attribute of a successful pattern. Crab flies must dive right-side up. If they land upside down, they must turn over in the water while sinking. Most of the crabs I bought when I was designing my pattern would not. I found out the hard way that permit will not eat something acting unnaturally. If I am spending a lot of money on a dream trip to a far-off destination, I don't want patterns that the quarry ignores. Testing is the last step, but a very important one.

Testing a pattern.

CHAPTER THREE

Fly-Tying Materials and their Properties

Threads

1. Dynacord RST 3/0 white—I use this for most applications. It is flat, very strong and not bulky.
2. Coats & Clark—This is clear nylon from a sewing shop. I use it for finishing off the heads of baitfish imitations when I want the underlying colors to show through. It isn't very strong, so I tie most of the fly with Dynacord and finish it with the monocord.

Hooks

1. Mustad AC 34068—This is the new Mustad "accupoint" hook with a triangular edge and a smaller barb. They have much better penetration than most other hooks I have used, but they are not totally rustproof and are nickel-plated.
2. Orvis 054960 3XL saltwater—I use these hooks on long-bodied patterns such as mantis shrimp and some streamers.
3. Dai-Riki 700B—This is a long-shanked hook with a bend in the shank that helps it ride upside down. I use it when tying crayfish, snapping shrimp, and other species that crawl on the bottom. It is not a saltwater hook, so care must be taken to rinse them after use.

Cement

1. Crazy Glue (industrial strength)—I use this to cement thread and materials as I tie the fly.
2. Five-minute Epoxy—This is used for finishing heads and cementing eyes to flies. It is strong and durable and it will produce a dimensional effect on eyeballs that is very realistic. It also adds weight to the pattern, so some care must be exercised in case the fly becomes unbalanced.
3. Worm plastic from Bass Pro—This is a very soft, clear plastic, which can be painted on shrimp bodies, etc. It can be dyed any color, but is very fragile. The good news is that it can be repaired easily with a hot spatula and more worm plastic.
4. Dow Corning RTV Sealant 734 Flowable Sealant—This is a self-leveling silicone rubber, semiclear and permanently soft and flexible. It is thinner than most silicone cements, so it is easier to work with. It can be used to coat the bodies of shrimp patterns and heads of baitfish patterns such as Eric's Cuda Slider, Pop Lips and Big Fish.

Eyes

1. Witch Craft Paste On Eyes from Witch Craft Tape Co.—These are lifelike eyes, easy to use, and very inexpensive. They come in all sizes and colors.
2. Bead-chain and Lead Eyes—I very seldom use these except on traditional bonefish patterns. If I want to weight the hook, I use flat lead under the body. Since I normally use either burnt mono or paste-on eyes that are more lifelike, I feel the others distract from the appearance of a pattern. Lead under the body makes less noise when entering the water. This is important on bonefish flats.

Latex Rub-R-Mold from Craft Shops

This is liquid latex used for legs, claws, and underbodies on crayfish, crabs, snapping shrimp, and mantis shrimp. It is also used to make tails and bodies for baitfish imitations. When cured, it is very tough and durable but also extremely flexible.

Body Material

1. Everglow Tubing—A hollow tubing that is iridescent. I use it for bodies on baitfish imitations. It has good flash, but isn't very durable; it needs to be coated with superglue for strength.
2. Lambs' wool on the hide—This hair has extremely good action in water, comes in all colors, but is not really durable. I use it for bodies on various shrimp patterns. It is also used for wings on streamers.
3. Egg Fly Yarn—This is a very fine synthetic yarn I use for bodies on crab patterns and wings on streamers. It has great action in water and comes in many colors. It does not absorb water as much as lambs' wool, and crabs are much easier to cast when the bodies are made of this material. It is very durable. It is an alternative to wool for streamer wings.
4. Mohair from yarn and weaver shops—This is a fuzzy yarn that comes in many colors. It is used for bodies on shrimp and baitfish patterns. It is very durable, and the fuzzy fibers protruding from the sides of the yarn give a very lifelike action. It also gives baitfish imitations a cylindrical bulk needed for round-bodied fish such as mullet.

Hair and Wing Material

1. Silk Brick from a weaver shop—This is very fine, raw white silk that comes in shanks. It is shiny, opaque and has unbeatable action. It is strong for its diameter, but it can't be considered really durable. It discolors easily, so flies tied with it must be washed in soapy water after use. I use it primarily for bellies on streamers.
2. Fish Fuzz (Craft fur, Fly fur) from Gurekes, Mystic Bay Flies, or craft shops—This is a very fine, synthetic hair and my favorite along with silk brick. It is translucent, durable and comes in many colors. It has super action, and I use it on all types of patterns.
3. Big Fly Hair—A very long, fine synthetic hair (ten inches), which I use primarily for very long streamers. It comes in many colors and is durable. It is not as fine as Fish Fuzz, but fine enough to have good action.
4. Fish Hair—This is a crinkly, stiffer, synthetic that is superdurable and is suitable for very large patterns.

Feathers

1. Schlapen—These feathers come from the backs of chickens and are used for the bodies of baitfish. When tied on whole, they have a wonderful undulating action. They are durable and come in many colors.
2. Saddle Hackle—These now come in many variegated colors that are perfect shades for simulating shrimp.
3. Hen Hackle—These are used for legs on shrimp patterns.
4. After-feathers—These are the small feathers found at the base of breast and other feathers on most birds. I use them for bodies on small baitfish patterns such as muddlers, gobies, blenies, and mud minnows. They have unbeatable action, but are very fragile.

Tinsel-like Material

1. Flashabou—A flat mylar in many colors. It is used to add flash to any pattern.
2. Crystalflash—A thin, crinkled, flashy synthetic material used like Flashabou, and is durable.
3. Fire Fly Tie—A bonded metallic nylon, somewhat similar to Flashabou, but with supposedly better action.
4. Glimmer—Much like Crystalflash, perhaps a little brighter.

Miscellaneous Material

1. Boars' bristles—Used for antennae on shrimp and crayfish; they are durable.
2. Lead Shot and Wire—Used for weighting crabs, shrimp, and crayfish.
3. Irrigation Syringes from your local dentist—Used for laying liquid latex on pictures of crabs, etc., to make legs, claws, tails, and bodies.
4. Marking Pens—Sharpies or Pantone can be used for coloring any pattern.
5. Acrylic Paint from artist supply stores—Used for mixing with liquid latex to achieve absolutely permanent colors.

CHAPTER FOUR

Fifteen Tying Techniques

The following is a brief description of fifteen tying techniques. Nine are suitable for various forage fish imitations. Three are single ties for crabs, sea urchins, mantis shrimp, snapping shrimp, juvenile lobsters, crayfish, swimming shrimp, shore shrimp, and grass shrimp. One is a suggestive tie for all shrimp species. The swimming, shore, and grass shrimp have been combined in one chapter, as have the snapping shrimp, lobsters and crayfish because of the similarities in the patterns. A tie for baitfish imitations called the yarnhead has been incorporated into the mullet pattern for the same reason.

A. Baitfish Techniques

1. Herring-shaped Fish

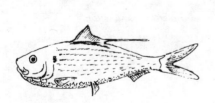

A simple line drawing of an Atlantic thread herring.

Atlantic herring.

21

This is a procedure to capture the shape of flat, thin baitfish that have deep bellies. The herring family is probably the most important food source for many of our backcountry and offshore gamefish. It is also a specific tie for the many freshwater members of the family. I have used it successfully for Atlantic salmon, rainbow and brown trout in Michigan, as well as for stripers, tarpon, snook, and redfish in the salt. The tie includes Fish Fuzz, silk brick, and Crystalflash to produce a lifelike imitation.

2. *Anchovies and Shiner-shaped Fish*

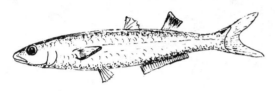

Atlantic silversides.

This is a tie for slender, streamlined baitfish, which include species of freshwater shiners, smelt, minnows, silversides, and dace. It is used on saltwater species to imitate grunion, top smelt, anchovies, sand lace, silversides, and ladyfish. When bay and striped anchovies are swarming among the 10,000 Islands of Florida, snook, jack crevalle, and tarpon become extremely selective, and this tie has worked very well for me. It combines silk brick, Fish Fuzz, egg fly yarn, and Flashabou to imitate both large fish and baitfish with this slim shape.

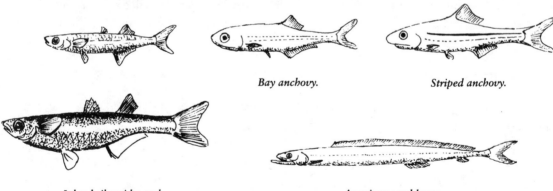

Bay anchovy.

Striped anchovy.

Inland silversides and tidewater silversides.

American sand lance.

3. Mullet-shaped Fish

This procedure is used to tie imitations of forage species with a round, stout, yet streamlined shape. I use it for striped and white mullet, and juvenile bonefish. Mullet are a staple of inshore and pelagic gamefishing worldwide. Young bonefish are actively sought after by barracuda and sharks on the flats. The tie combines various hairs, Flashabou, Crystalflash, and mohair yarn to achieve a robust shape.

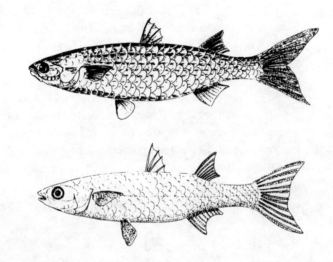

Striped and white mullet.

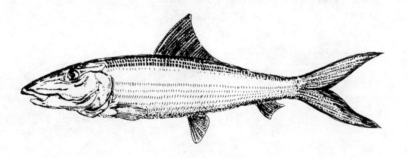

Bonefish.

4. *Yarnhead*

This is an alternative tie for mullet and bonefish that is very realistic. I will incorporate it in the mullet chapter. It adds a latex tail and a clipped egg yarn-head with hair behind the head.

5. *Glass Minnows*

Glass minnow.

This is a pattern for the so-called glass minnows found in all tropical and subtropical inshore waters. They are small, often tiny, fish thought to be young of the year of anchovy and sardine species. A good imitation is vital when this type of prey is swarming around lighted docks and bridges at night. Huge schools annually migrate up coastal rivers in the fall to escape cold water and are heavily fed upon in both instances. This a simple, but realistic and effective, pattern to tie using only Fish Fuzz, eyes, and Crystalflash to achieve the effect.

6. *Pin Fish, Butterfish, Bluegill-shaped Fish*

This is a method of achieving wide bodies that a variety of forage exhibit. It is suitable for tilapia, pin fish, blue-gills, perch, and butterfish, to name just a few. It incorporates various hairs, Crystalflash, and mylar tubing to sim-ulate a wide, robust shape.

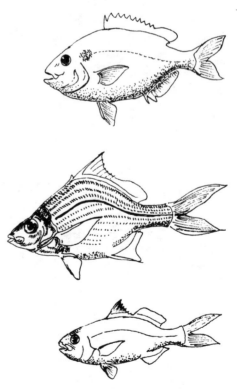

Pin fish, striped majorra, and spot-finned majorra.

7. Schlapen Technique

A method of using schlapen with hair to tie medium-to-large baitfish imitations of fish with both slender and robust bodies. It includes hair and Crystalflash in the design.

8. Latex Tails

This procedure is used to add tails to streamer flies. It is especially useful when imitating fish with tails that are large in relation to their bodies. I have used it on species such as rainbow smelt, mullet, bonefish, and ladyfish. The supple latex tails are durable and impart wobbly swimming motions to the flies.

9. Latex-bodied Fish Imitations

This technique allows very close imitations of fish that have elaborate markings on their bodies such as spots, bars, and stripes. Intricate designs can be painted on the latex bodies to produce results that could not be created with fur and feathers alone. I use it to imitate species of gobies, blenies, darters, cusk eels, snake eels, freshwater sculpen, mud minnows, and young trout. Like the latex tail, the body imparts an intriguing action in water.

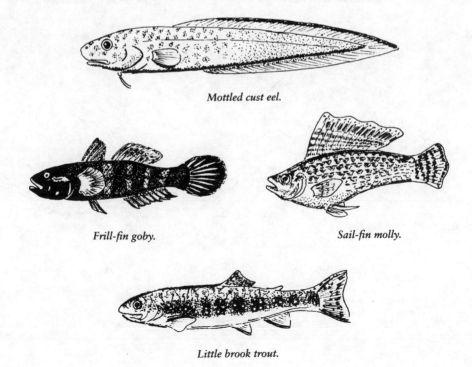

Mottled cust eel.

Frill-fin goby.

Sail-fin molly.

Little brook trout.

B. Invertebrate Techniques

1. Crabs

This is my tie for all crab species using liquid latex for the claws, legs, and the underside of these crustaceans—these are superlifelike and have excellent swimming action. They are effective for all fish that eat crabs. This dressing looks difficult to tie, but it isn't.

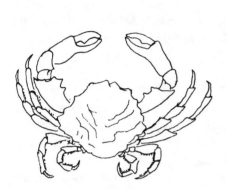

Green Reef Crab

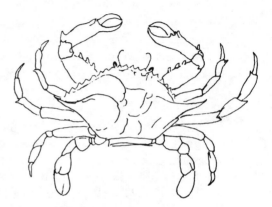

Common Blue Crab

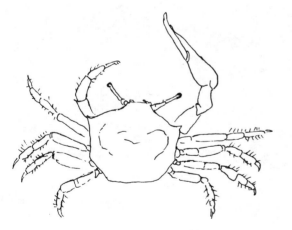

Fiddler Crab Mate

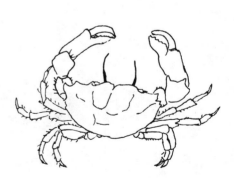

Mangrove Mud Crab

Humpbacker Red Spotted Spider Crab

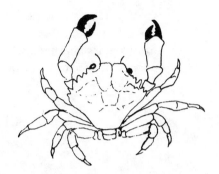

Florida Mud Crab

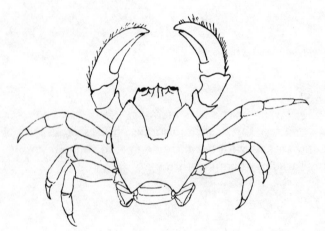

Porcelin Crab

Spotted or Black-Fingered Mud Crab

2. *Snapping Shrimp, Lobsters, Freshwater Crayfish*

This is a realistic tie for snapping shrimp, crayfish, and young lobsters. Bottom feeders such as bonefish, redfish and permit consume large amounts of these types. Of course, freshwater crayfish in the soft-shelled stage is the preferred bait for smallmouth bass and trout. The tie includes the use of liquid latex and hair such as sheep fleece and Fish Fuzz in the dressing.

3. Swimming Shrimp

An easy but realistic tie for commercial swimming shrimp, grass shrimp, and shore shrimp that both bottom feeders and pelagic fish eat. The tie combines various hairs and hackle along with burnt mono eyes to produce deadly flies for specific species of shrimp.

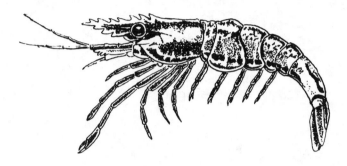

Swimming shrimp.

4. Shrimpy

Another easy tie and a suggestive pattern for all shrimp species. It uses variegated shades of saddle hackle and mohair with burnt mono eyes to simulate the shapes and hues of the many varieties of natural shrimp.

5. Mantis Shrimp

This is a time-consuming pattern, but superrealistic and very effective. It combines various hairs, mono eyes, and latex pinchers to produce a great dressing that really produces on bottom feeders.

6. Sea Urchins

A very easy tie, but at the same time accurate, that uses deer hair for the spines and liquid latex for the test. Permit and bonefish eat these bottom dwellers regularly.

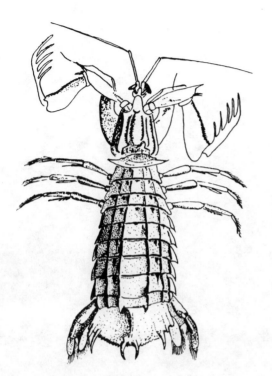
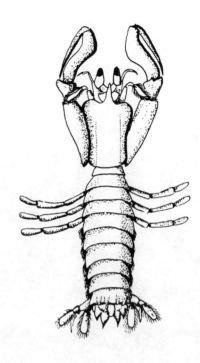

Two types of mantis shrimp.

CHAPTER FIVE

Tying Spanish Sardines and Scaled Sardines (Herring-shaped Fish)

The imitation described in this chapter is specific for Spanish sardines and scaled sardines (*Sardinella anchovia* and *Harrengula pensacolae*). It can be adapted to most members of the family with little or no modification. These fish are found in both fresh and salt water. They are a schooling fish, and when schools are found, heavy feeding by gamefish can take place. Other important herring species include the Atlantic thread, Alabama shad, Gulf menhaden, gizzard shad, hickory shad, alewife, American shad, and Atlantic herring. Spanish and scaled sardines are similar and often mistaken for each other. The Spanish has no shoulder spot and the back is a little fatter. The scaled sardine often has a dark humeral spot. Both are small, silvery fish with deep bellies, thin from side to side, and greenish above. When a bright light is shined on them at night, an electric green line fluoresces from the eyes to the tail on the mid-dorsal line and a yellow-gold strip shines below the green back. Both species live inshore and are found along the beaches to areas far inside bays and estuaries. *S. anchovia* ranges from Massachusetts to Bermuda, the Gulf Coast, the Caribbean, and Brazil. The scaled sardine is found from Florida, the Gulf of Mexico, and the Caribbean to Brazil. They grow to six inches.

Scaled sardine.

This pattern has taken striped bass in Cape Cod, redfish, snook, jack cravelle, and tarpon on Florida's west coast, and snook and tarpon at Casa Blanca on Mexico's Ascension Bay.

In fresh water, I have landed Atlantic salmon, rainbow, and brown trout with them. If I had to pick one streamer for the largest variety of gamefish under all conditions, this would be it. I tie the pattern from one-and-a-half to six inches long. The smaller sizes are required when fishing around lighted docks and bridges at night in the spring and summer for snook and tarpon, and in fresh water for trout. The lights attract huge schools of sardines that attract the predators. Under these conditions a close imitation is always necessary. The larger sizes are used for most species of saltwater gamefish in the daytime, and stripers, blues, and bonito off Cape Cod beaches at night.

The usual retrieve for the pattern is short, fast twitches. This summer I discovered, more by accident than design, a novel retrieve while fishing for tarpon in a lagoon near Ascension Bay. The fish were rolling high, which is a sure sign they were diving deep after the roll. The tarpon ignored the normal retrieve, but when I made a cast to a spot where a roll was and let the fly sink, I would jump a fish every time. They were hitting the fly on a dead-sink, with no action except the waving of the hair and silk as it drifted down. I hooked nine tarpon that day. The same lagoon was fished each day during the week by other guests at the lodge with very little success. These fish wanted sardines, and they wanted them deep.

Spanish Sardine—Materials

HOOK	Mustad AC 34068 #3/0 to #6.
THREAD	3/0 Dynacord and transparent Coats & Clark.
REAR WING	Polar-bear-colored Fish Fuzz.
BODY	Hollow, pearlescent Everglow tubing.
FRONT UNDERWING	Polar bear Fish Fuzz, over which is tied white silk brick.
OVERWING	Polar bear Fish Fuzz under ivory glow-in-the-dark Flashabou; under green Fish Fuzz; under gold Flashabou.
SIDE	Two strands of pearlescent Krystal Flash.
GILLS	One strand of red glow-in-the-dark Flashabou.
EYES	Large press-on eyes.
CEMENT	Five-minute epoxy and Crazy Glue.
WEIGHT	Lead wire optional; this is sometimes used on the New England coast when fishing for stripers or blues.

Spanish sardine.

Tying Instructions

1. Tie in a batch of polar bear Fish Fuzz at the bend of the hook so it slopes slightly down from the horizontal. This is to help create the deep belly.
2. Tie in a cylinder of Everglow tubing at the bend and wrap to the head.
3. Tie in a thin batch of Fish Fuzz under the hook at the eye so it extends back to the bend.
4. Tie in a bunch of silk brick on either side of the Fish Fuzz under the hook. This procedure completes the deep belly, which is opaque, glistening white.
5. Tie in a batch of polar bear Fish Fuzz on top of the hook at the eye to extend back to the end of the hair that was tied in at the bend of the hook.
6. Switch the thread to the transparent Coats & Clark and tie in five strands of pearl Flashabou (this glows green in the dark).
7. Tie in a small batch of green Fish Fuzz over the Flashabou.
8. Tie in a smaller batch of gold Fish Fuzz over the green.
9. Tie in two strands of pearlescent Crystalflash on either side of the body at the midline to extend the entire length of the body.
10. Tie in one short strand of red glow in the dark Flashabou on either side of the body in the gill position.
11. Tie off head and cement with five-minute epoxy.
12. Paint two paste-on eyes with a thin layer of yellow acrylic paint and draw a black line around the outside of the eye.
13. Place the eyes on the top of the head (see ill. for correct position).
14. Paint five-minute epoxy on the eyes and head, being careful to use only enough to keep the eyes firmly cemented. As I am tying the pattern, I cement each step with Crazy Glue for durability. If you paint Crazy Glue on the head or eyes, you must wait a day before you place the epoxy since they will react with each other and become too gummy.

Step 1   *Step 2*

(Tying instructions for Spanish sardine continued on next page.)

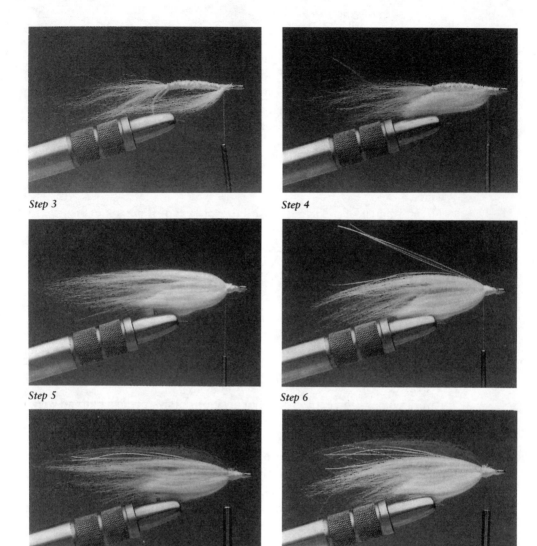

Step 3

Step 4

Step 5

Step 6

Step 7

Steps 8–11

Steps 12–14

CHAPTER SIX

Tying Shiners, Anchovies, Sand Lace, and Silversides (Slim-shaped Fish)

This is a realistic method for tying patterns to imitate any baitfish with a slim, streamlined shape. I will explain ties for the freshwater black-nosed shiner (*Notropis heterolepis*), the saltwater bay anchovy (*Anchoa mitchilli*), American sand lace (*Ammodytes hexapyerus*), and Atlantic silversides (*Menidia menidia*). With little modification, these patterns are close imitations of similar-shaped species such as freshwater smelt, dace, minnows, shiners, and silversides. Color plates for most can be found in *Peterson's Field Guide to Fresh Water Fishes*. The method is appropriate for saltwater forage such as striped anchovies, long-nosed anchovies, Pacific anchovies, tidewater silversides, and top smelt. Color plates of many of these fish can be found in *Peterson's Guide to Atlantic and Pacific Coast Fishes*, but, as always, it is much better to take your own. The black-nosed shiner is a freshwater minnow common in the northern United States and Canada to areas 400 miles west of the Mississippi River. Its habitat is clear lakes, creeks, and small rivers. Its appearance is, for fly-tying purposes, identical to many other shiner and minnow species. This is also a killer pattern for landlocked salmon in Michigan.

The bay anchovy is a prolific inshore fish. It grows to four inches and lives in shallow bays, estuaries, and passes. Its range is from Maine to Florida and the Gulf of Mexico. They school in large numbers and are attracted to lights. The very small imitations have taken large snook and tarpon in the 10,000 Islands.

Sand lace, called sand eels on Cape Cod and in Long Island Sound, are very long, very thin fish with olive dorsals, and silver-white sides. They have a bright olive-gold stripe along the mid-dorsal line. They reach eight inches and range from Quebec to North Carolina They are circumpolar—also found in the North Pacific—but these may be a separate species.

Atlantic silversides are a long, silvery fish with a bright silver stripe down the mid-dorsal, and a oliveish tan or greyish dorsal with orange pectoral fins. They reach six inches and range from the Gulf of St. Lawrence to northeastern Florida. Along with sand lace, they are found along sandy beaches and the mouths of inlets, and often swarm together.

The reef silversides is deadly on bonefish and most other gamefish found around bonefish flats. For all practical purposes, it the same tie as the Atlantic silversides and they are very close in appearance.

All of these imitations are usually fished with short medium-speed strips. This is the way the naturals mill around. When frightened, however, they dart about rapidly, so this type of retrieve sometimes pays off.

Black-nosed Shiner, Bay Anchovy, Sand Lace, Silversides—Materials

HOOK	Orvis 3x1 saltwater or Mustad AC 34068 #2 to #6
THREAD	Transparent Coats & Clark
BODY	None
UNDERWING	White silk brick under white Fish Fuzz
OVERWING	a. Black-nosed shiner—tan lambs' fleece under black Fish Fuzz under tan Fish Fuzz under dirty-olive Fish Fuzz
	b. Bay anchovy—polar bear Fish Fuzz under gold Fish Fuzz
	c. Sand lace—greenish olive Fish Fuzz
	d. Silversides—tan big fish hair under brown Fish Fuzz or green Fish Fuzz under brown Fish Fuzz
SIDE TINSEL	a. Silversides and bay anchovy—silver Flashabou
	b. Black-nosed shiner—pearlescent Crystalflash
	c. Sand lace—yellow-gold Crystalflash
EYES	Small paste-on silver with black pupil

Tying Instructions

All of these patterns can be tied using long-shanked or regular-length hooks. I use the regular length when I want a larger gap for fish like snook, which have large mouths. With the regular-length hooks I use a tail wing, like on the Spanish sardine. With the long, shanked hook, I eliminate it.

Black-nosed Shiner, using long-shanked hook

1. Wrap thread on hook at eye and take it one-quarter of the way back to the bend.
2. Tie in a bunch of silk brick on the underside of the hook so it extends back to the bend.
3. Tie in a slim bunch of tan lambs' fleece on the side of the hook to extend beyond the bend, about the length of the body.
4. Tie in a bunch of black Fish Fuzz on top of the tan fleece.
5. Tie in a bunch of tan Fish Fuzz over the black.
6. Tie in a bunch of dirty-olive Fish Fuzz over the tan.
7. Tie in a single strand of pearlescent Flashabou along the side at the midline on each side.
8. Place small paste-on eyes in the middle of the head and cement the head and eyes with five-minute epoxy.

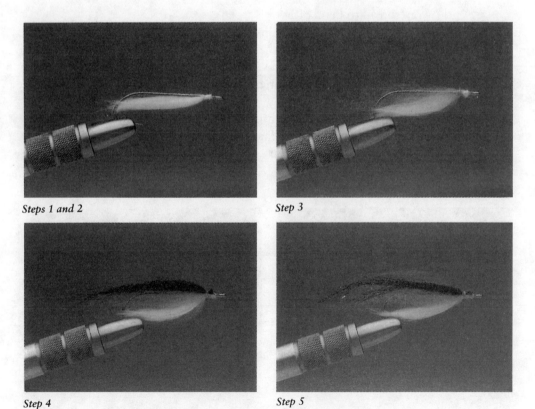

Steps 1 and 2

Step 3

Step 4

Step 5

Tying procedure for black-nosed shiner (continued on next page)

Steps 6 and 7　　　　　　　　　　　*Step 8*

Silversides, using regular-length hook

1. Wrap thread to bend of hook.
2. Tie in a bunch of light gray Fish Fuzz to top of the hook.
3. Take thread to just behind the eye and tie in a bunch of silk brick on the underside of the hook so it extends back to the bend.
4. Tie in the tan Big Fly Hair on top of the hook to extend as far back as the tail hair.
5. Tie in a very slim bunch of brown Fish Fuzz over the tan.
6. Tie in one strand of silver Flashabou on each side at the midline.
7. Place the eyes on the top part of the head and cement the head and eyes with five-minute epoxy.

Steps 1 and 2　　　　　　　　　　　*Step 3*

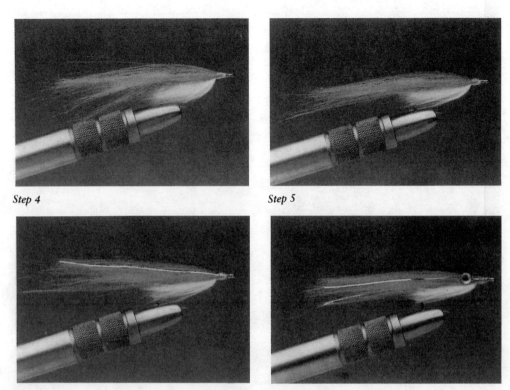

Step 4   *Step 5*

Step 5   *Steps 6 and 7*

Tying procedure for silversides (continued from preceding page).

A sand lance.

CHAPTER SEVEN

Tying Bonefish, Mullet, and Latex Tails (Round-bodied Fish)

These dressings are imitative for robust, round-bodied yet streamlined fish. They are specific for white mullet, striped mullet, and young bonefish. The white mullet has a white belly, silvery sides, and is blue or olive-gray on the back. It exhibits a small dark spot at the pectoral fin and the operculum has a gold spot. The eye possesses a narrow vertical line. They are found in water saltier than striped mullet's and spawn in the spring. There is a migration of white mullet along the Florida coast; northward in the spring, and south in the fall. These movements create heavy feeding by gamefish.

They are found in the eastern Pacific and Atlantic Oceans and in the western Atlantic from Massachusetts to Brazil. They can attain a length of two feet but we tie them from three inches to seven inches. The striped mullet has a silver body with black stripes and a black back. They exhibit a large black spot at the pectoral fin. The eyes are brownish with a black pupil. The younger the fish, the lighter the stripes. Striped mullet are fall spawners. They are found in water from fresh to salt and are abundant in the backcountry of western Florida. They inhabit all temperate and tropical waters around the world.

Bonefish are silvery with bluish or greenish reflections on the back, with dark streaks on the upper half of the body. The young, which we are imitating, are sandy above with nine narrow gray-tan crossbars, and silvery below. They can grow to forty-one inches, but I am imitating five-inch to eight-inch juveniles. They are found in all tropical areas.

Fabien Johnson with a nice barracuda taken on a baby bonefish imitation.

All gamefish except bottom feeders eat mullet. The striped mullet are always around shallow bays of the 10,000 Islands and in coastal lakes, which may be fresh or brackish water. Tarpon and snook are also in these areas and they take this imitation well.

Sharks and barracuda roam the same flats that bonefish feed upon and they really like young "bones."

The imitations for bonefish and mullet can be fished at speeds very fast, medium, or slow. Barracuda like very fast retrieves; shark, tarpon, and snook will hit flies worked more slowly.

White Mullet, Bonefish—Materials

HOOK	Mustad AC 34068 #3/0 to #2
THREAD	Dynacord 3/0 white
BODY	White mohair
UNDERWING	White silk brick and white Fish Fuzz
WING	Fish Fuzz in polar bear, light yellow, and black
TAIL	Latex (optional)
PECTORAL FINS	Silver pheasant breast feathers
EYES	Large paste-on eyes
LIQUID LATEX	This for the optional tails

Striped Mullet—Materials

TOP WING	Brown and black Fish Fuzz
EYE TINT	Brown acrylic paint
SIDE STRIPS	Black Flashabou
PECTORAL FINS	Black body feathers from a silver pheasant

The other materials are the same as for the white mullet.

Tying Instructions

Constructing Latex Tails

Make a copy or drawing of a tail the correct size and shape for the fish you are going to imitate. Any of the field guides will help. Place tape over the drawing; this makes it easier to remove the tail after it cures. Cut a piece of nylon (about twenty-pound test) about ten inches long and tape it to the drawing so it extends from the base of the tail toward the head. Take a disposable irrigation syringe, fill it with Rub-R-Mold liquid latex, and inject a thin layer over the drawing and the nylon. Let it cure for seventy-two hours at 72°F. Heat will greatly accelerate curing. The latex will still stick to itself, even when cured, but soaking it in water will alleviate this tendency. Turn the tail over and inject more liquid latex on the mono for strength. Mix some acrylic paint and liquid latex the color of the tail of the species you are tying and paint the tail using a paintbrush. White mullet have medium-gray tails, striped mullet have very dark tails, and bonefish have very light tanish gray tails. You can mix the latex and paint in the beginning, before you load the syringe, and eliminate the painting steps if you wish. Once the tail is completed and cured, it should be coated with Armor-All to keep it supple.

Copy of a tail with mono taped to it.

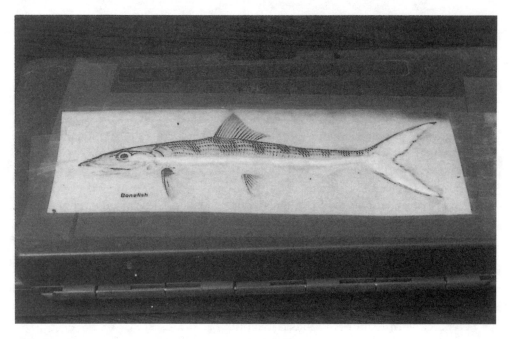

Latex over the copy.

Injecting latex on the other side of the mono.

Painting the tail with a marking pen. You can also use latex mixed with acrylic paint.

Tying Procedure for White Mullet

1. Tie in a bunch of polar bear Fish Fuzz at the bend of the hook.
2. Tie in the prepared tail over the Fish Fuzz.
3. Tie in more Fish Fuzz over the tail.
4. Wrap white mohair yarn for the body. (Mohair yarn has numerous fibers extending out from its body. Be careful not to wrap them down, as they are needed to create the round bulk that the bodies of these fish have.)
5. Tie in some white Fish Fuzz on the underside of the hook, extending to the bend.
6. Tie in white silk brick on either side of the Fish Fuzz.
7. Tie in some polar bear Fish Fuzz on top of the hook to extend back to the tail. At this point, switch to the transparent thread.
8. Tie in a small bunch of yellow, then gray Fish Fuzz.
9. Tie in three strips of Crystalflash on the sides.
10. Take two silver pheasant flank feathers, trim the butts and cement them into the hair wings.
11. Tie off the head and place the eyes.
12. Paint a vertical line on the iris with gold paint.
13. Cement the eyes and the head with five-minute epoxy.
14. Place the gold-and-black markings on the body with marking pens.

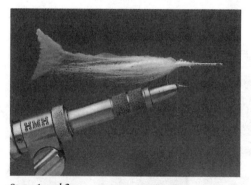

Steps 1 and 2

Step 3

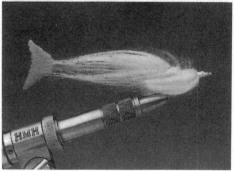

Step 4

Step 5

Step 6

Step 7

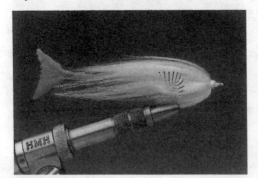

Steps 8–10

Steps 11–14

Bonefish

The only difference from the above is the markings. Tan vertical bars are placed over the dorsal with a marking pen and gray iridescent strips of Crystalflash are tied along the sides to represent the horizontal lines.

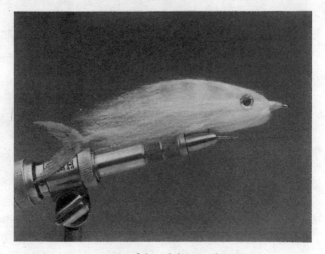

Bonefish with latex tail.

Striped Mullet

A striped mullet with a latex tail.

This is the same tie, except the topping is brown and black. Three black spots are placed behind the eye, which is tinted with light brown acrylic paint. The dark strips on the sides are simulated by tying in eight or ten black strips of Crystalflash. This is the very best pattern I have ever found for tarpon in the backcountry.

Yarnhead Mullet and Bonefish

A frill-finned goby with a latex tail.

This is another method of achieving the robust shape of these fish. It uses egg fly yarn for the head and front one-third of the body. The same materials are used, except yarn is spun on the hook in the manner of the Wool-head Muddler, after the tail and wings are tied in. I use egg fly yarn because it does not absorb water as much as wool, so it is easier to cast.

CHAPTER EIGHT

Tying Glass Minnows

Glass minnows are thought to be the young of anchovies and sardines. They have silvery transparent bodies with big eyeballs. The really noticeable feature is the eyeballs. They school in spring, summer, and fall, and are attracted to snook lights. There is a fall migration up coastal rivers in Florida. These forage are only 1/2-inch in the spring and perhaps 11/2- to 2-inches in the fall migration. Gamefish feed on them at all stages due to their huge numbers.

I used to think these small flies were most useful fished under lights at night for snook and tarpon, but I got a big surprise last March in Belize while fishing for bonefish. I was at a new camp called the Golden Bonefish Lodge, on Cockney Cay. It is owned, managed, and guided by Fabien Johnson and his younger brother William, who are the two best guides in the country. The bonefish were plentiful, with many large ones, but very picky. No one pattern was consistent, so, after much switching with little success, I decided to try something unconventional. *Bonefish are not thought to eat* very many small fish but I had noted schools of very small white mullet and glass minnows in shallow water near the beach around the lodge. I tied on a 3/4-inch glass minnow pattern and cast to the next school I came across. Bingo! First cast, a nice 4-pounder. One fish from the next two schools also took on the first cast. After releasing the third fish, I made a blind cast to a likely looking grass patch and quickly connected to a 5-pound mutton snapper. That was so much fun I continued blind-casting and it seemed I couldn't make a cast without getting a strike. I soon lost track of the number of fish I landed, but I kept track of the different species. That afternoon I took both small and large bonefish, five species of snapper, four species of jacks, and four different grunts. I would have had another species, but the barracuda kept biting through the leader. Fabien, my guide for that day, remarked, "Mon, you catching some nice fish there. Those are good eating fish. Too bad we didn't bring a bucket—we could use them back at camp." My suggestion of making a stringer out of a piece of heavy nylon was quickly rejected. "Mon, sharks come and eat them." These little glass minnows raise big fish and even bones, which are not supposed to take baitfish.

The imitations can be fished just under the surface with short slow strips when they are used under the lights for snook, tarpon and jacks. When I was at the Golden Bonefish Lodge and had so much success blind-casting, I was fishing the first flat inside the outermost reef (Turneffe Reef). There I made long casts and retrieved with short, quick strips so the fly was close to the surface. When I, or more likely Fabien or William, spotted a bonefish, I would cast just ahead of the fish, let the fly sink, and when the bone reached the fly I would use quick strips, but with varying intervals between them. This is a deadly pattern for bonefish and many other species. Do not neglect it because of its small size.

Glass Minnows—Materials

HOOK	Mustad AC 340068 #6 to #8
THREAD	Coats & Clark transparent
WING	Polar bear Fish Fuzz
EYES	Paste-on

Tying Instructions

1. Tie a slim bunch of white or light polar bear Fish Fuzz just behind the eye, under the hook to extend a little beyond the bend.
2. Tie the same material on top of the hook.
3. Tie off and place the eyes in the middle of the head.
4. Cement the eyes and head with five-minute epoxy.

When tied in larger sizes than one inch, you can add a topping of light tan Fish Fuzz over the white. One piece of pearlescent Crystalflash can be added to the sides for a little flash if desired.

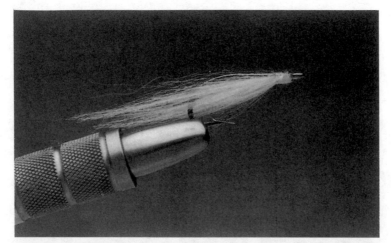

Step 1

Step 2

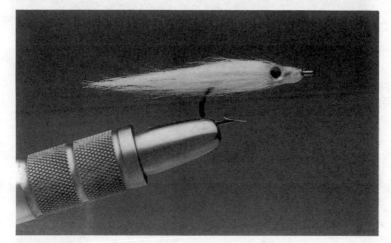

Steps 3 and 4

Tying instructions for a glass minnow.

CHAPTER NINE

Tying Pin Fish and Mojarra (Bluegill-shaped Fish)

This is a method of tying bluegill-shaped baitfish. Many species have this shape, both in freshwater and saltwater. I will describe a pin fish (*Lagodon rhomboides*) tie. These are a favorite bait for snook, tarpon, and redfish in the Florida Keys and the 10,000 Islands.

The pin fish is one of the most common inshore fishes. They are found from Massachusetts and Bermuda to Florida and the Gulf of Mexico. They may reach ten inches and give the impression of a wide-bodied, silvery fish with bluish reflections. They have yellow fins and a dark brown spot behind their golden eyes. Adult fish have six vertical bars along the sides.

Last summer I took a 40-pound tarpon in a shallow bay within sight of Marco Island Bridge on this pattern. I used a medium-fast retrieve with a pause every three or four strips. I will vary the speed if I am not getting strikes.

Pin Fish—Materials

HOOK	Mustad AC 34068 #1/0 to #6
THREAD	3/0 white Monocord and Coats & Clark transparent
TAIL	Yellow latex (optional)
BODY	Pearlescent Everglow tubing
WING	Polar bear Fish Fuzz
TOPPING	Gold Fish Fuzz
SIDE STRIPES	Gold and blue Crystalflash
EYES	Paste-on eyes painted gold

Tying Instructions

1. Tie in polar bear Fish Fuzz at the bend of the hook.
2. Tie in tail, it you take this option. The tail is made first as described in Chapter 6.
3. Tie in more polar bear Fish Fuzz over the tail.
4. Tie in the Everglow and wrap it to the head.
5. Tie in enough Fish Fuzz on the underside of the hook to form a deep belly.
6. Tie in enough Fish Fuzz on top of the hook to form a deep back.
7. Tie in a small batch of gold Fish Fuzz over the top of the back.
8. Tie in three fibers of blue Crystalflash along the sides so they are as widely separated as possible.
9. Tie in ten fibers of gold Crystalflash along the sides so they are as widely separated as possible.
10. Tie off the head and paint the eyes with yellow-gold acrylic paint (thin coats; too much paint and the silver glitter will not show through).
11. Cement the head and eyes with five-minute epoxy.
12. Paint the dark spot behind the eye with a brown marking pen.

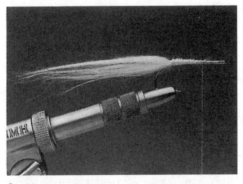

Step 1

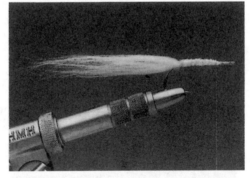

Steps 2–4

Step 5

Step 6

Tying instructions for pin fish.

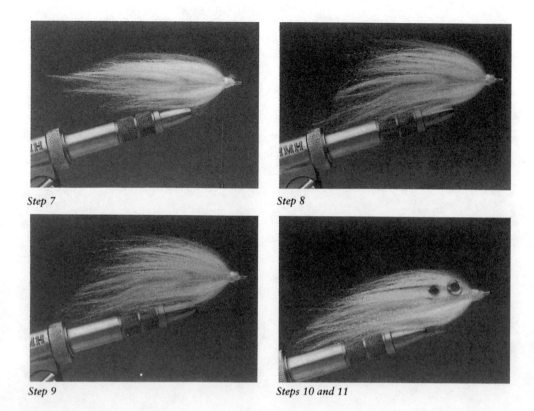

Step 7

Step 8

Step 9

Steps 10 and 11

Other Species with this Shape

There are hundreds of other species of baitfish with this shape which can be imitated with this tie. Refer to the various field guides for the colors if you do not have your own pictures.

CHAPTER TEN

Tying Spot-finned Mojarra (Schlapen Technique)

This is a method of using schlapen feathers when dressing baitfish patterns. It is possible to simulate thin, thick, and wide-bodied species with these feathers, which have an enticing action in water. I will demonstrate the pattern for the spot-finned mojarra (*Eucinostomus argenteus*), and of course the materials can be modified to tie any medium-size baitfish. Mojarra are elegant, silver fish with high backs, protrusible jaws and grow to eight inches. The range is from New Jersey to Bermuda, through the Caribbean, Gulf of Mexico, to Brazil. They are a common inshore baitfish, and the imitation is very good on tarpon and snook in southwest Florida. I usually fish it with a medium-fast retrieve, but when tarpon are rolling high and diving deep I let it sink, and often get strikes as it nears the bottom.

Spot-finned Mojarra—Materials

HOOK	Mustad AC 34068 #1/0 to #6
THREAD	Coats & Clark
WING	White schlapen
SIDES	Polar bear Fish Fuzz and pearlescent yellow Crystalflash
EYES	Paste-on, large for the size of the body

Tying Instructions

1. Wrap the thread on the hook and take it one-quarter of the way back to the bend.
2. Tie in two schlapen feathers (white) on each side of the hook. These should be the length of the fly you are tying; I like them two to five inches long.
3. Tie in a bunch of polar bear Fish Fuzz on each side of the schlapen. This is about one-half the length of the feather. In this case keep it thin. If you were tying a round-bodied fish, you would tie it in thicker.
4. Tie in two strips of yellow Crystalflash on either side of the body, and as long as the body.
5. Tie off the head, place the eyes, and cement the head and eyes with five-minute epoxy.

Steps 1–3

Step 4

Tying procedure for spot-finned majorra.

Step 5

CHAPTER ELEVEN

Tying Little Brook Trout
(Latex-Bodied Technique)

T his is a method of tying intricately patterned and colored fish of any shape. I use it in fresh water to imitate small trout, mud minnows, sculpins, perch, trout perch, bluegills, dace, shiners, top minnows, killfish, sailfin mollies, and darters. In the salt, I use the tie for gaily colored species of wormfish, gobies, blennies, pin fish, grunts, snappers, and cusk eels.

The posterior two-thirds of the body, dorsal fin, tail fin, and caudal fins are flat latex that can be painted any color and any design needed to imitate the natural.

I will explain the dressing of a little brook trout, which big brown love to eat. A few years ago I was fishing the Au Sable River in Michigan during a midge hatch when I hooked a small brook trout. As I was bringing it in, a huge brown trout came out of nowhere and ate it whole. I let the brown have slack line, but as he swam off the leader parted. Another time, Jim Wakley (a famous guide on the same river), told me about an experience he had on the South Branch. His client caught an eight-inch brookie and put it in the live well. Jim landed a seventeen-inch brown and also put it in the live well. Upon arriving back at the dock, they noticed the brookie had disappeared. When they cleaned the brown, they found the brookie in its stomach. I decided if big browns like little brookies that much I would certainly try to give them what they wanted. This imitation works especially well when the smaller fish are engrossed in feeding on the hatch and the cannibals are cruising the pools, looking for a mouthful.

Little Brook Trout—Materials

HOOK	Mustad AC 34068
THREAD	3/0 white Dynacord
BODY AND FINS	Rub-R-Mold liquid latex
FRONT BODY	Olive and white Fish Fuzz
EYES	Paste-on
PAINT	Liquid acrylic mixed with liquid latex

Tying Instructions

1. The latex body is fabricated first. This is the same procedure as preparing and painting the latex tails. See Chapter 6 for the details. Once the body is cured, it can be painted with the bars, stripes, and spots of the natural. It is then coated with Armor-All to keep it supply, and tied on at the bend of the hook.

Fabricating the latex body.

Tying on the latex body to the hook (step 1).

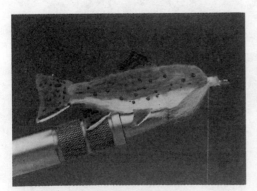

Adding the white Fish Fuzz (step 2).

Step 2

Step 3
Tying procedure for brook trout.

Steps 4 and 5

2. Tie white Fish Fuzz under the hook eye and olive Fish Fuzz on the sides
   so it extends one-third of the length of the body.
3. At this point, you may add a little flash by tying a few strands of Crystalflash to the sides.
4. Tie off the head and place the eyes on the head.
5. Cement the head and eyes with five-minute epoxy.

A little brown trout with a latex body.

When I am tying a species that lives on the bottom, such as sculpin or mud
minnows, or in salt water, gobies and blennies, I tie the pattern weighted so it
will ride upside down. I tie a flat lead strip on the tip of the hook, and then I
can fish the fly on the bottom and make it swim like the natural.

CHAPTER TWELVE

Crabs

Tying Crabs (Atlantic Mole, Black-fingered Mud, Casa Blanca Blue, Green Reef, Pacific Mole, Common Blue, and Smooth Porcelain)

This tie also uses liquid latex in reproducing the claws, legs, and underside of the natural. The anatomy of the belly, which is distinctive, can be replicated precisely and this is the shape you should be imitating. The legs and claws shimmy and waggle so they have excellent action. Any species can be imitated with this tie, but I have the most experience with green reef (*Mithrax sculptus*), common blue (*Callinectes sapidus*), casa blanca blue (*Callinectes marginatus*), black-fingered mud (Family *Xanthidae*), Pacific mole (*Emerita analoga*), Atlantic mole (*Emerita analoga*), and smooth porcelain (*Petrolisthes politus*) crabs, since they are the most common in the areas I fish.

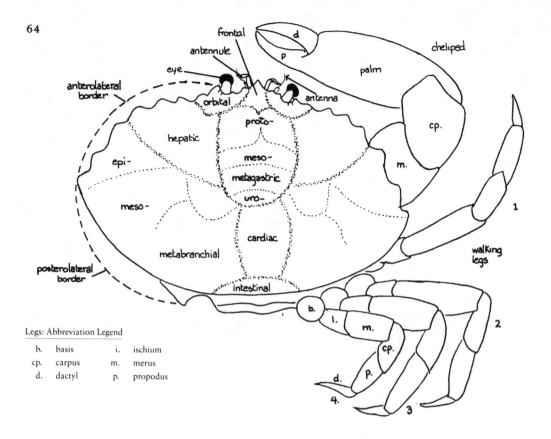

Legs: Abbreviation Legend

b.	basis	i.	ischium
cp.	carpus	m.	merus
d.	dactyl	p.	propodus

Abbreviation Legend

b.	basis
cp.	carpus
cx.	coxa
d.	dactyl
end.	endognath
ex.	exognath
i.	ischium
m.	merus
p.	propodus

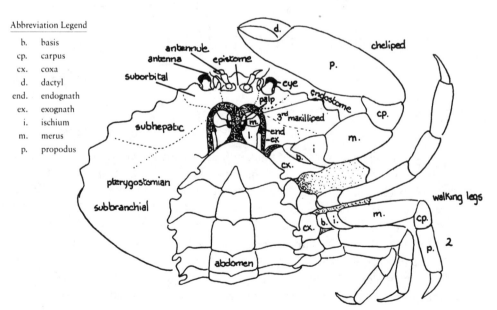

Anatomy—top and bottom—of a crab.

All bottom feeders take crabs, especially permit, redfish and bonefish, but most gamefish will eat them if they get the chance.

Descriptions

Atlantic Mole Crab

Appearance Carapace creamish with tanish mottling. Underside, white with yellow reflections. Legs, white. Antennae, white or cream, long and feathery. Length, to 1¼ inches.

Habitat Open, sandy beaches between high and low tide lines, in surf in "swash" zone.

Range Cape Cod to Florida, Texas, and Mexico.

Comments Tarpon, snook, and other gamefish feed on these crabs just off the beach. They move up and down the beach in the swash zone, with the tide, and are constantly being uncovered by the waves.

Black-fingered Mud Crabs

Appearance Carapace mottled tan, brown, black, generally resembling a clump of dead oyster shells. Underside, dirty cream to tan. Legs, same as carapace.

Habitat Muddy bottoms, mangrove roots, especially in and around oyster bars.

Range Massachusetts to Brazil, West Indies, Bahamas.

Comments These small crabs are a favorite of redfish and bonefish in mangrove lagoons.

Casa Blanca Blue Swimming Crab

Appearance Carapace mottled purple, tan and yellow. Tips of claws, blue. Underside, orangeish tan.

Habitat Shallows and brackish estuaries.

Range Mexico to Brazil, especially prevalent in the Yucatan and Ascension Bay, Belize.

Comments This is the tropical version of our edible blue crab. It is the pattern to use if you are traveling to Ascension Bay for permit.

Common Blue Swimming Crab

Appearance This is the color of the juvenile's carapace, from sand with slight purpose aspects, to tan, to gray-green to brown. Legs, variable, from pure sand to highly colored with orange, blue, yellow, and red. Grows to 9½ inches.
Habitat Shallows and brackish water to 120 feet.
Range Nova Scotia to Florida, Texas, Bermuda, West Indies, to Uruguay.
Comments This is a very common crab in Florida.

Green Reef Crab

Appearance Carapace olive green with darker green rounded ridges in a definite pattern. Legs, brown and hairy. Claws, dark green. Underside, a little lighter green than the top. To 1 inch long.
Habitat Reefs, turtle grass beds, shallow flats.
Range Florida, Bahamas, West Indies, to Brazil.
Comments This is a very important species on which bonefish feed heavily in the Bahamas or shallow flats during a rising tide. They are numerous in Belize and on Turneffe Reef.

Pacific Mole Crab

Appearance Carapace pale tan or gray with purple overtones, underside white. Antennae, gray with blue stalk and very long and feathery. To 1 inch long.
Habitat Open sandy beaches between high and low tide lines, in swash.
Range Alaska, to Peru and Chile.
Comments Often found in dense concentrations on sandy beaches. This is the imitation for corbina in California.

Smooth Porcelain Crab

Appearance Carapace, cylindrical; mottled tan, dark brown and black with long, tan antennae. Only three legs visible on each side. Grows to 1½ centimeters.
Habitat Lives under intertidal rocks and in oyster beds.
Range North Carolina through the Caribbean, to Brazil.
Comments I have collected this species around mangrove islands in southwest Florida. They can be seen by the thousands at low tide and, despite their tiny size, they seem to be the main diet of the redfish in the area.

I will detail the procedure for the Common Blue Swimming Crab. This pattern can be fished diving to the bottom, walking on the bottom, or swimming just below the surface in tidal flows.

Common Blue Crab—Materials

HOOK	Mustad AC 34068 2/0 to 8
THREAD	3/0 white Monocord
LEGS, BELLY, AND CLAWS	Liquid latex
CARAPACE	Sand-colored egg fly yarn
EYES	Burnt mono

Tying Instructions

1. The claws, legs, and underbelly are prepared first in the same manner as the latex tails; see Chapter 6 for details. The crab is more difficult to work with because all the legs tend to stick together even after they have cured. If you soak the cured latex by laying a wet paper towel on it for a few minutes, it will turn white and separate more easily. You then allow the latex to dry out flat and it will lay out perfectly. The curing time can be shortened considerably by placing it in a warm oven.

Constructing the claws, underbelly, and legs.

The latex is laid down on alternative segments to create a jointed effect. This also helps to keep the legs from being stiff, as they are thinner at the segments.

2. Place the hook in the vise and tie a strip of egg fly yarn at the bend of the hook, on top, and parallel to the shank. Tie it on the hook in the middle of the yarn and wind two tight winds, then take the thread to the front of the yarn and wrap two more tight wraps just in front of the original wraps. Continue this to the eye of the hook. This is very similar to tying an egg fly or a wool-head muddler.

3. Tie off the head, fluff with a toothbrush, and clip the top to the shape of a blue crab, which is twice as wide as it is long.

4. Place Crazy Glue on the head and under the thread but not the yarn.

5. Make the burnt mono eyes by holding eighty-pound test mono in a lighter until it is the correct size and place them in the carapace. Cement with five-minute epoxy. You can also add feelers if you wish.

6. Take a lead splitshot, flatten it with a hammer, and cut it to the shape of the front half of the body.

7. Paint a little liquid latex on the underside of the body and lay the lead on the body—let the latex harden for about a half hour and press the lead down so it is flat and as close to the body as possible.

8. Place more liquid latex on the entire underbody and over the now-attached lead. Place the legs and latex body on the liquid latex and allow it to cure.

9. Paint the claws and latex belly with a little acrylic paint mixed in with liquid latex. The underside of a blue crab is white. You will need a picture to paint the legs because they are variable, depending on age.

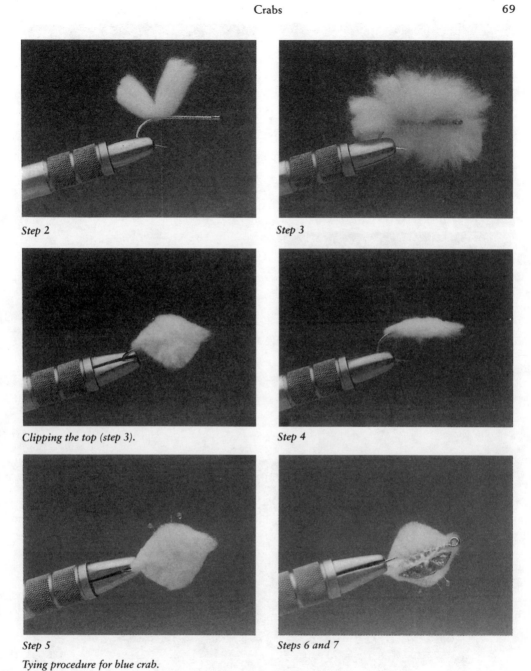

Step 2

Step 3

Clipping the top (step 3).

Step 4

Step 5

Steps 6 and 7

Tying procedure for blue crab.

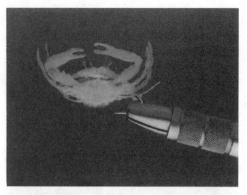

Step 8

Step 9, underside

Painting the underside of a blue crab with a mixture of liquid latex and acrylic paint.

Marking the carapace with a marking pen.

Constructing a mold.

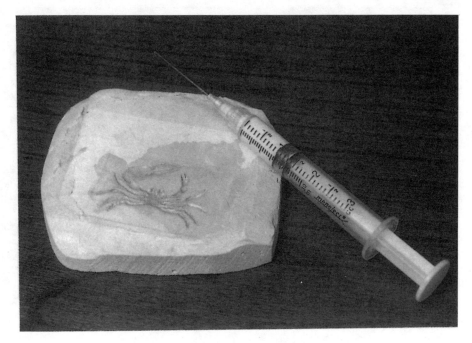

The mold ready to use.

Basically, you are now done. The claws will lie flat, and if you wish to have them in the attack position you can pin them in that position and paint a little latex on the bend. Allow it to cure and the claws will stay in this position. After the legs are done, it is very important to paint them with Armor-All to keep them supple.

A variation of this tie is to paint the top of the carapace with liquid latex as well as the bottom; this looks and feels very natural.

I have just recently captured, photographed and am raising a number of green reef and other spider crab species. Until now, I was never able to obtain a good photograph of these crabs and now that I have my own shots, I see a unique problem in duplicating them. They have extremely hairy legs and significantly raised dumps on the carapace. These features are visually striking, so an imitation lacking these features does not achieve a good simulation of the natural. Because the green reef crab is such a significant food source for permit and bonefish, I feel it is important to incorporate them into the pattern.

Here is how I create these features in the fly.

1. After the latex underbody and legs have been prepared in the usual manner, color them green with a marking pen and paint a little more liquid latex on the legs, but not the claws.
2. Cut a bunch of creamy tan elk hair into little, short pieces and sprinkle it over the latex. When the latex dries, the hair will adhere to the legs.
3. Turn the legs over the repeat the procedure. I use elk hair on this species because the hairs are coarse. Any dubbing fur, natural or artificial, can be used, depending on the desired effect.
4. The conspicuous bumps on the carapace can be added after the crab is complete by mixing dark green acrylic paint with some liquid latex and placing it on the top of the body. These bumps are in a definite pattern, so you will need a good photo to go by. The color of the bodies of the naturals varies from light to dark; the larger the crab, the darker the carapace. In any case, it is not one solid shade and this should be taken into account when imitating the species.

This imitation was tied to ride hook-down and that is the way I prefer to fish them, but you can tie them to ride hook-up if you wish. They turn over better if they are tied to ride hook-down. My feelings on this are the following: if I am fishing in sand or mud, I want the hook to dig in so when I strip the fly back, a little puff of bottom material will be created. If I am fishing in grass, I need a weed guard, and hook-up will not help. If I am fishing over rock or coral, hook-up is good as long as the fly will actually turn over when it lands upside down. None of the flies I have purchased in fly shops will do this. I very seldom fish over coral but even then a weed guard works. When I do tie these with a weed guard I prefer the double-wire type. They are much more efficient, especially in grass, than the other types.

When fishing for permit, I want two weighted types. One should be weighted as explained in the tying instructions. This is the slower-sinking version. It is used when permit are tailing in shallow water with the bonefish. I also use it for redfish and sheepshead. When permit are in deeper water, three to four feet, I want a faster-sinking crab. I weight this one by flatting a split-shot with a hammer so as to get a round shape, and I hammer it so one side is thin and the other is thicker, like a wedge. The thick end is attached to the front of the body, where the eyes are, so the crab dives headfirst. When I spot a permit in deeper water, I cast it in front of the fish and let it sink.

Hopefully, the fish will take it on the sink or as it lies on the bottom. If it doesn't, I strip the crab back with short, quick strips. If the permit are tailing, I do not lead it; instead I cast directly at the tail and let it sink.

CHAPTER THIRTEEN

Tying Snapping Shrimp, Crayfish, and Spiny Lobsters

S napping shrimp, freshwater crayfish, and spiny lobsters all have a sim-ilar shape, so imitations can be made for all three using the same tech-nique with a little variation in size and color. Snapping shrimp are a saltwater version of the freshwater crayfish and are consumed by bonefish, permit, redfish, and other bottom feeders with the same gusto as soft-shelled crayfish are taken by bass and trout.

Author with a nice Belizean bonefish on a pink snapping shrimp.

There are more than 240 species of freshwater crayfish known to North America and the colors vary considerably. Most anglers are familiar with them, especially the ones found in their own area. The species I am familiar with is the Midwest Crayfish (*Orconectes rusticus*). The hard-shell stage appears very dark brown with black markings, but under close examination has light tan, orange, red, and cream in the body and legs. The soft-shell stage is a little lighter and is more greenish. The fish definitely prefer greenish imitations.

Snapping Shrimp

Snapping shrimp look very much like crayfish except they have only one large claw. There are similar saltwater crustaceans called mud shrimp and ghost shrimp, but all can be imitated with the same tie. The colors of all of these are variable and usually takes on the bottom are never one solid color. They usually have one major ground color, then spots, mottling, or banding of other colors which, even when bright, contribute to camouflage the animal. Local knowledge is very helpful when tying imitations, as many species exist worldwide. Permit seem to like these shrimp as much as they like crabs, probably because they are a very rich food source.

Snapping shrimp make a distinct noise when the lock mechanism of the large claw releases. The claw snaps shut creating a sound like a pistol shot. This sound can be simulated by incorporating a worm rattle in the body of the imitation.

Young spiny lobsters (*Panulirus argus*) are similar in shape to crayfish and snapping shrimp except they have no large claws. Permit and other gamefish eat them regularly.

The most common species of snapping and sponge shrimp are listed with their color, range and habitat.

Snapping Shrimp (*Alpheus* species)

Common or Big-clawed Snapping Shrimp
(A. heterochaelis)

Color Dark transparent green flushed with purple on the sides of the carapace with white markings on the first two pairs of legs. Walking legs, pale red, tips of tails blue with a narrow border of orange on the distal margin. The outer part of tail, red just above the blue and a narrow white border. The joints of abdominal segments, white. Can be 40 to 50 millimeters long.

Habitat Broken shell, stones, or burrows in mud; shallows to 30 meters.

Range Chesapeake Bay to Brazil; very common in the 10,000 Islands of Florida.

Banded Snapping Shrimp (A. armillatus)

Color Dark brown ground color crossed by nine elliptical bands of translucent white, equal in width to intervening dark bands. Carapace with three white bands, the third one at the posterior margin. The abdomen with six bands, the first blending with the last on the carapace. Walking legs, pink or brown with cream bands. Tail fan has a broad brown crossband at edge.

Variations Abdomen often dark green with spots bordered by a line of orange. Tail with broad crossband tipped with orange. Chelae thickly speckled with dark gray, whiteish bands above tipped with pink. Walking legs, orange-yellow, banded with white. Two other color phases, one a blue-gray similar to the common snapping shrimp and one a straw yellow. Grows 40 to 45 millimeters long. Eggs, black.

Habitat Under rocks, shells, in holes in rocks, turtle grass, in shallow water to 14 meters.

Range North Carolina through the Gulf of Mexico; West Indies, Bermuda, to Brazil. They are very numerous in the Bahamas and Florida and are a preferred forage of bonefish in these areas.

Red Snapping Shrimp (A. armatus)

Color Bright pink to red with white widely spaced spots and a lateral line. Antennae, red-and-white banded, walking legs blue to reddish blue. Claws pink-to-red with white spots and tiny red dots. With white at segments. To 38 millimeters long.

Habitat Lives beneath tentacles of ringed anemone near reefs in shallow water.

Range Florida, West Indies, and Caribbean. Pink snapping shrimp are my preferred imitation for bonefish in the Bahamas and the Yucatan. Size #2 for Bahamas and #6 for the Yucatan.

Green Snapping Shrimp (A. normanni)

Color Gray or dark green, often mottled with dark green or brown, a paler spot beneath each eye. Large claw, dark green, banded with yellow-brown or yellow on inner surface, small claw and other legs paler, banded with dull gray. To 30 millimeters long.

Habitat Shelly or rocky bottom, in burrows, in sand, in shallow water, mud flats, and turtle grass, and among reef coral. This is a very common and numerous species.

Range Chesapeake Bay through the Gulf of Mexico, to Brazil, Gulf of California, and Panama.

Striped Snapping Shrimp (A. formosus)

Color Ground color yellow or greenish brown, finely speckled with orange, and a narrow light stripe alone the mid-dorsal line from just behind the eye to the tip of the tail. The line is light orange anteriorly changing to yellowish green and finally gray near the tail. Brown stripe on each side dorsolaterally and below this another stripe of white. Or, colors similar to dorsal stripe along each side followed by a stripe of dark reddish brown and another stripe of blue bordering the abdomen. Antennules and walking legs, blue. Tail white at base, blotched and bordered with yellow. To 40 millimeters long.

Habitat Sand and mud flats, rock-studded beaches, sea walls, and exposed and submerged reefs from above low tide line to 42 meters.

Range North Carolina through Gulf of Mexico, to Brazil, West Indies, and Bermuda.

Sponge Shrimp (Pistol shrimp)
(*Synalpheus* species)

Red-Speckled Sponge Shrimp (S. fritzmuelleri)

Color Claws green, darker toward extremities of fingers. Body colors speckled with tiny red chromatophores. A subspecies (*S. f. elongatus*), claws and second leg, blue; anterior part of claw, light green.

Habitat Lives in sponges, reefs, crevices, and jetties from low to 50 meters.

Range North Carolina to Brazil, Bermuda, south Atlantic; Baja, California.

Long-clawed Snapping Shrimp (S. longicarpus)

Color Translucent white, fingers brown. To 22 millimeters long.

Habitat Lives under shells, rubble, coral, or the interior of sponges.

Range North Carolina to Texas, Yucatan, Mexico, West Indies, to Brazil.

Yellow Sponge Shrimp (S. minus)

Color Body is translucent yellowish white; large claw, white or gray, fingers orange, tips red, banded near base of fingers with white in female. The body is spiral, dotted with green chromotophores. Tips of third maxillipod and distal one-third of first pair of chelae bright pink, eggs green. To 38 millimeters long.

Habitat Sponges, coral, shells, stones, grass flats, intertidal to 85 meters.

Range North Carolina to Brazil; Bermuda.

Small Snapping Shrimp (S. townsendi)

Color Body and legs translucent pinkish red; large claw pink, changing to green on fingers.

Habitat Sponges, reefs, low tide line to 102 meters.

Range Gulf of Mexico, Bermuda, Gulf of California.

Short-clawed Sponge Shrimp (S. brevicarpus)

Color Light green with red-tipped large claw; or orange with blue walking legs, cream swimerets, light bluish cream antennae.

Habitat Inside sponges.

Range Florida, Gulf of Mexico, Caribbean, Bahamas.

I will give the instructions for the dressing of the red snapping shrimp and then explain the variations to tie freshwater crayfish and juvenile Spiny Lobsters.

Red Snapping Shrimp—Materials

HOOK   Mustad AC 34068 or Dai-Riki 700-B #2 to #8
THREAD   3/0 Dynacord

CLAWS	Rub-R-Mold liquid latex
ANTENNAE	Boars' bristles
EYES	Burnt mono
ROSTRUM AND CARAPACE	Pinking red Fish Fuzz or sheep fleece
WALKING LEGS	Long, stiff fibered cock hackle dyed blue
SWIMMING LEGS	Short, pink, webby hackle
ABDOMEN	Same as carapace
TAIL	Same as carapace
RATTLE	Worm rattle

Tying Instructions

1. Construct claws using the same procedure as the tails—see Chapter 6.
2. Tie in burnt mono eye at the bend of the hook sloping down, away from the shank. This pattern is tied to ride upside down.
3. Tie in the antennae so they will be coming from under the eyes, double

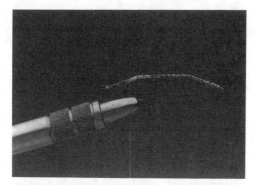

Step 2

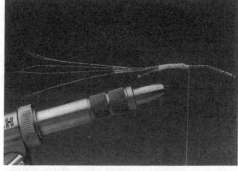

Step 3

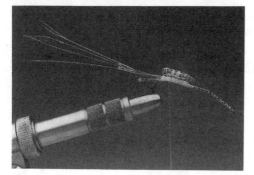

Step 4

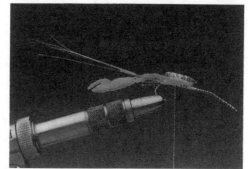

Step 5

Tying procedure for red snapping shrimp.

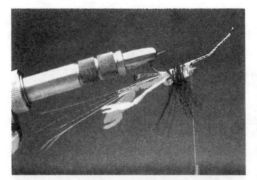

Step 6

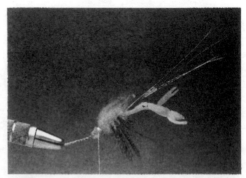

Step 7a

Step 7b

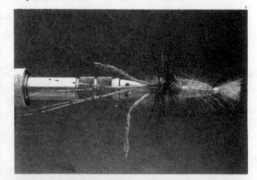

Steps 9–11, bottom view

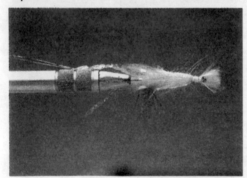

Steps 9–11, top view

Step 12

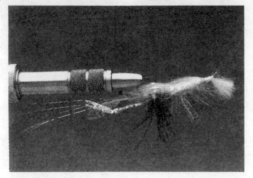

Steps 13 and 14

in this case—that is, two from each side. You can tie one strand of Crys-talflash on each side for a little flash in dark conditions; I usually cut it off on sunny days.

4. Tie in a worm rattle at the bend on top of the hook.

5. Tie in the prepared claws.

6. Wrap a large bluish-red hackle just behind the claws to one-quarter of the way to the eye of the hook and clip the top fibers.

7. a) Tie in a bunch of reddish Fish Fuzz behind the blue hackle to form the head and carapace. b) Tie in a short-fibered pink saddle hackle, wind to eye, tie off and clip off the top and side fibers.

8. If you want more weight than the worm rattle, you can tie in a lead eye on top of the hook at the eye.

9. Tie in a bunch of pinkish Fish Fuzz on top of the hook to form the abdomen and tail.

10. Bend the fibers protruding in front of the hook eye above the eye, making four figure-eights, and tie off.

11. If you can tie the tail a little off-center, it will cause the pattern to jump sideways as you work it over the bottom. This seems to be attractive to gamefish.

12. Paint the head with five-minute epoxy, eject some latex over and around the belly (worm rattle), and paint the latex with Armor-All.

13. Color the antennae with red and white bands, with a permanent marker, or latex.

14. Paint the diffuse white spots on the thorax and the carapace with liquid latex mixed with white acrylic paint.

Freshwater Crayfish and Spiny Lobsters

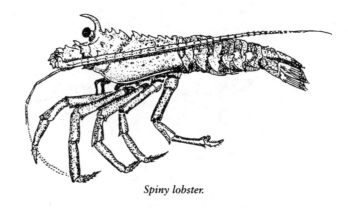

Spiny lobster.

The same technique and materials with very little modification can be adapted to imitate crayfish and spiny lobsters. Crayfish have two large claws and spiny lobsters have none. Lobsters have much longer and thicker antennae, and these can be imitated with turkey or goose tail and wing fibers. If more thickness is necessary, add layers of latex until the desired effect is attained. When the natural you are imitating has designs on the carapace and abdomen like the banded snapping shrimp, I paint these on with Tulip Colorpont Paintstitching or colored liquid latex.

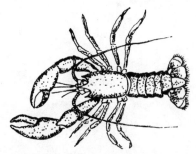

Freshwater crayfish.

(top) Spanish sardine
(bottom) Glass minnow

Spanish sardine
(collected from Marco Island, Florida, area)

Butterfish (collected from Martha's Vineyard)

Scaled sardine
(collected from Venice Inlet, Florida)

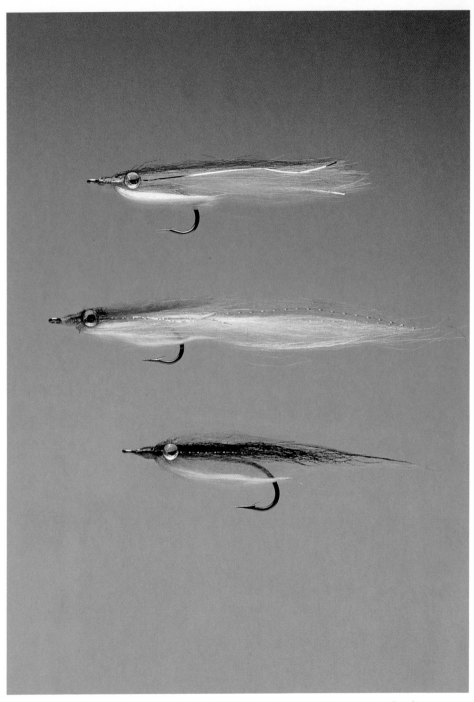

(top) Atlantic silversides, (middle) American sand lance (sand eel),
(bottom) Blacknosed shiner

Atlantic silversides
(collected from Martha's Vineyard)

American sand lance
(collected from Martha's Vineyard)

Blacknosed shiner
(collected from Silver Lake, Michigan)

Sail-fin mollys
(collected from the Blackwater River, Florida)

(top) Striped mullet
(bottom) Young bonefish

Striped mullet
(collected from Naples, Florida, area)

(top) White mullet
(bottom) Frillfin goby

Goby species
(collected from flats near Turneffe Reef)

Striped majorra
(collected from the
Blackwater River, Florida)

Spot-finned majorra
(collected from Goodland, Florida, area)

Mud minnow
(collected from the Rogue River, Michigan)

Pinfish
(collected from Marathon, Florida, area)

(top) Little brook trout
(bottom) Little brown trout

(top left) Blue crab (immature), (top right) Green reef crab,
(middle) Pacific mole crab, (bottom left) Black-fingered mud crab
(bottom right) Smooth porcelain mud crab

Green reef crab (collected from Turneffe Reef)

Juvenile blue swimming crab
(collected from Port of the Islands, Florida)

Smooth porcelain crab
(collected from Port of the Islands, Florida)

Black-fingered mud crab
(collected from Everglades City, Florida, area)

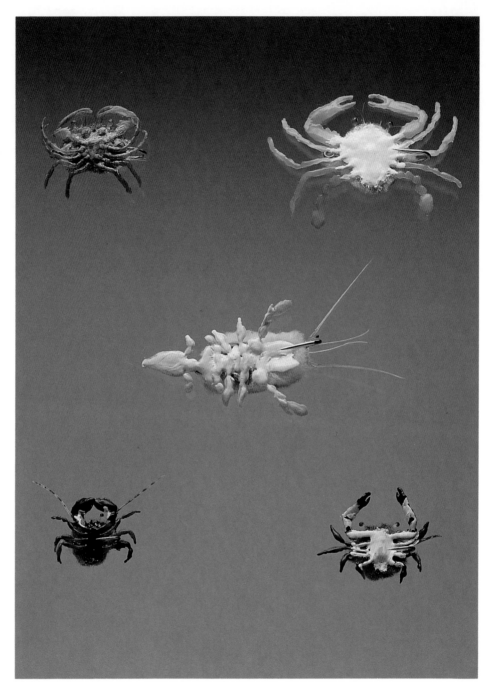

UNDERSIDE OF:
(top left) Green reef crab, (top right) Blue crab (immature), (middle) Pacific mole crab, (bottom left) Smooth porcelaïn crab, (bottom right) Black-fingered mud crab

Cream mantis shrimp
(collected from Turneffe Reef)

Dark green mantis shrimp
(collected from Turneffe Reef)

Banded snapping shrimp
(collected from The Berry Islands)

Brown snapping shrimp
(collected from intertidal zone,
Cockney Key, Belize)

Pink snapping shrimp
(collected from intertidal zone, Cockney Key, Belize)

Mantis shrimp
(collected from the Florida Keys, Marathon area)

(top) Golden mantis shrimp
(bottom) Pink snapping shrimp—aka red snapping shrimp

(top) Spiny lobster, (bottom) Freshwater crayfish (soft-shelled phase)

Spiny lobster (collected from Ascension Bay, Mexico)

Soft-shelled crayfish
(collected from the Big Manistee River, Michigan)

(top) Hair shrimpy
(bottom) Feather shrimpy

CHAPTER FOURTEEN

Tying Commercial Swimming Shrimp, Grass and Shore Shrimp

S wimming shrimp are the type found in shrimp cocktails. Grass and shore shrimp are small shrimp that are similar in appearance to the larger swimming shrimp. There are three species of swimming shrimp in our area: White (*Penaeus setiferus*), Brown (*P. aztecus*), and Pink (*P. duorarum*). All spawn offshore and move inshore to bays and estuaries at the postlarval stage, where they grow rapidly to maturity. The growth is from 1.5 to 2 millimeters per day. When they reach 70 to 100 millimeters, they undertake mass migrations from the backcountry to the outside. At these times gamefish feed on them selectively and heavily. These shrimp are especially important to fly fishermen because they mature in the shallow areas where we do most of our fishing. Also, the outward migrations present gamefish with tremendous feeding opportunities and us with some of their fastest action of the year. I have taken tarpon, snook, redfish, ladyfish, snapper and bonefish on the pattern I will describe. It can be fished on the bottom medium-slow, midlevel with short, quick strips, or just subsurface, drifting with the tidal race.

The following is a description of each species.

White Swimming Shrimp

Color Juveniles and young adults, ground color is light gray with slate blue or brown spots widely spaced except on the sides, ridges, and tails, where they

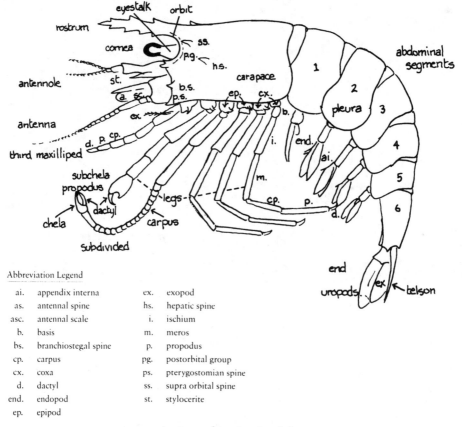

Abbreviation Legend

ai.	appendix interna	ex.	exopod
as.	antennal spine	hs.	hepatic spine
asc.	antennal scale	i.	ischium
b.	basis	m.	meros
bs.	branchiostegal spine	p.	propodus
cp.	carpus	pg.	postorbital group
cx.	coxa	ps.	pterygostomian spine
d.	dactyl	ss.	supra orbital spine
end.	endopod	st.	stylocerite
ep.	epipod		

Anatomy of a swimming shrimp.

are denser, giving the effect of tiger stripes on the abdomen. If the shrimp come from grass beds, they have a greenish hue. The antennae rostrom, blades of pleopods, and tips of tails are marked with pink to reddish brown. To 100 millimeters long.

Range Cape Cod to the Caribbean, and the south Atlantic.

Habitat Juveniles, shallow backcountry bays and estuaries.

Brown Swimming Shrimp

Color Juveniles and young adults, extremely variable; brown or grayish brown with darker spots, some red and some green individuals.

Range Cape Cod, Caribbean, to South America.

Habitat Juveniles, shallow backcountry bays and estuaries.

Pink Swimming Shrimp

Color Juveniles and young adults, extremely variable; gray, reddish brown, or bluish gray with a distinct spot of darker color at the middle of the abdomen. This spot and banding can be gray, blue gray, blue, or purple. The tail fan is transparent edged with purple.

Range Cape Cod, Carribbean ,to South America.

Habitat Juveniles, shallow backcountry bays and estuaries.

The eyes of these swimming shrimp have a golden yellow pupil that glows like neon when it is illuminated. This is only apparent on fresh, healthy specimens, and is especially visible at night. The brain and stomach, which are just behind the eyes, are visible through the translucent carapace, which is black with gold reflections at night.

This pattern is ideal for the imitation of other types of shrimp that have the same general shape. These include shore shrimp, grass shrimp, sand shrimp, boreal red shrimp, arrow shrimp, and some cleaning shrimp.

This pattern is for the white swimming shrimp, which is the most common species in the 10,000 Islands and the Florida Keys.

White Swimming Shrimp—Materials

HOOK	Mustad AC 34068 or Dai-Riki 700B 3/0 to 8
THREAD	3/0 white Dynacord
WEIGHT	Flat lead wire (optional)
EYES	Burnt mono
ANTENNAE	Boars' bristles
CARAPACE AND ABDOMEN	Light gray sheep fleece of Fish Fuzz
ROSTRUM	Tan hackle turkey biot
WALKING LEGS	Long, light brown cock hackle
SWIMMING LEGS	Short, tan webby hackle
ANTENNAL SCAL, ANTENNUL, AND STYLOCERITE	Speckled tan and brown hackle tips (these look like a lower lip below the eyes, but are really the base of the various antennae).

Tying Instructions

1. Tie in burnt mono eyes.
2. Tie in four speckled hackle tips under eyes to extend a little beyond eyes.
3. Tie in turkey biot over and between eyes.

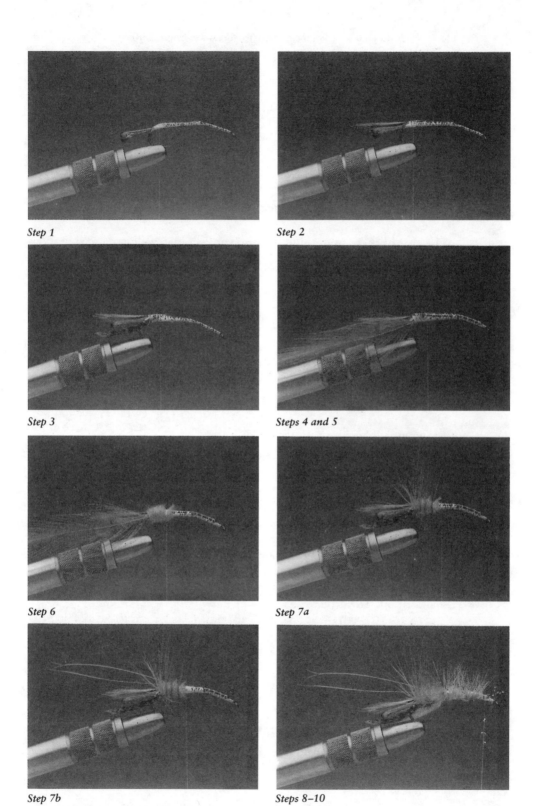

Step 1

Step 2

Step 3

Steps 4 and 5

Step 6

Step 7a

Step 7b

Steps 8–10

Tying procedure for white swimming shrimp.

Step 11

Steps 12–14

Steps 15 and 16

4. Tie in a long cock hackle at the bend of the hook.
5. If you want the pattern weighted, tie in one or two pieces of flat lead on the top of the hook shank, as this pattern is designed to ride hook-up.
6. Tie in and wrap a little bump of gray mohair yarn just behind where the hackle is tied in.
7. Wrap hackle back toward the eye of the hook and tie off.
8. Tie in antennae below the eyes.
9. Clip hackle on the top, which is the bottom of the hook shank.
10. Paint the hump of yarn black and gold, this representing the brain and stomach.
11. Tie in a bunch of gray Fish Fuzz or sheep fleece behind the brain on the bottom of the hook to form the carapace.
12. Tie in a short, tan webby saddle hackle behind the carapace and wrap to the eye of the hook and tie off. Clip it both top and sides.
13. Tie in another bunch of Fish Fuzz or sheep fleece at the eye of the hook so it extends to the carapace and beyond the hook eye.

14. Pull the tail part of the hair down and fasten it down with tying thread.
15. Cement head with five-minute epoxy and paint the pupils of the eyes metallic gold with a tiny black dot in the middle.
16. Paint in the tiny brown or black dots with a fine-tipped marking pen.
17. Paint the antennae and edges of the tail fan red.

CHAPTER FIFTEEN

Tying Mantis Shrimp

This pattern is as close to an exact imitation as I can get. It is the most complex and time-consuming of all the patterns, but I believe the extra effort is well worth it. I will suggest a simpler pattern I have developed that is quite effective.

Tim Fox with a Belizean bonefish on a mantis shrimp.

91

Mantis shrimp do not look like shrimp, but closely resemble the praying mantis insect. Mantis shrimp are bottom dwellers found in all seas, from shallow flats to deep reefs. They are fed upon by bonefish, permit, redfish, and sheepshead. A more simplistic imitation of the Golden Mantis has taken three world-record bonefish off Bimini. These shrimp are often gaily colored with intricate designs, and even the species that appear drab at first glance exhibit these features when closely examined. There are hundreds of species worldwide, but the most common exist in the Gulf of Mexico, South Atlantic, Bahamas, and the Caribbean. Their characteristics are as follows:

Golden Mantis, False Mantis
(Pseudosquilla ciliata)

Color Extremely variable; yellowish brown, greenish brown, bright green, pale green, or whiteish. To 4 inches long.

Habitat In burrows, coral reefs, and grass beds in shallow water.

Range South Florida, Bermuda, Bahamas, West Indies, to Brazil.

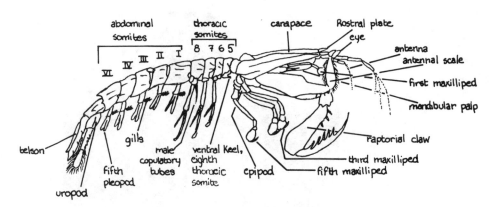

Anatomy of a mantis shrimp.

Common Mantis (Yellow Mantis)
(Squilla empusa)

Color Whiteish with yellow-to-orange body ridges, or greenish with darker green and blue margins. Eyes, green. To 10 inches long.

Habitat Burrows in sand and mud from low tide line to 500 feet above line.

Range Cape Cod to Florida, Texas, south to Brazil.

Rock Mantis (Gonoductylus oerstedii)

Color Black with cream mottling, or cream with light green mottling, or dark green with cream mottling, or cream with tan mottling. To 3 inches long.

Habitat Coral rock from low tide line to shallow water.

Range Florida, Bahamas, to Venezuela.

These are the thumpers rather than the slashers. They are extremely numerous on Turneffe Reef and probably many other areas. I recently had the opportunity to fish with Fabien Johnson, the owner of the Golden Bonefish Lodge and one of the most gracious hosts and, along with his brother William, the best guide in Belize. We walked the reef at low tide together collecting prey species. Hundreds of mantis shrimp could be seen darting in the shoals. These shrimp were not hiding in holes as I had supposed rock mantis would. They were swimming in short, speedy bursts in the clear, shallow water. All four color phases were present in the same area and Fabien wished I had an imitation of them. When I said I did, and showed him my fly box of mantis, he said, "Mon, put that on, we catch those bones." So I did, and we did.

Scaly-tailed Mantis (Lysiosquilla scabricauda)

Color Cream with dark brown segmented crossbands.

Habitat Burrows in sand and mud in shallow water.

Range Florida to Texas, West Indies to Brazil.

I will give the tying instructions for the Golden Mantis. This pattern is balanced, so when it is retrieved it will face its attacker and jump backward on the bottom, just as the natural acts. If the tail is slanted sideways, it will jump sideways. This action is very attractive to bonefish.

Golden Mantis—Materials

HOOK	Dai-Riki 700B #2, #4, #6
THREAD	3/0 white Dynacord
EYES	Burnt mono
ANTENNULE	Base nylon tippet material; ends, three boars' bristles on each antennule
ANTENNAE	Turkey-wing fibers
EARS	Latex on nylon tippet material
RAPTORIAL LEGS	Latex
WALKING LEGS	Long, stiff, cream cock hackle
CARAPACE AND ABDOMEN	Cream Fish Fuzz or sheep fleece
SWEMMERETTS (PLEOPODS)	Short, webby, badger hackle
TAIL	Same as carapace or latex
WEIGHT	Flat lead strips or lead eyes

Tying Instructions

1. Prepare the raptorial legs and the ears. The legs are constructed the same way the latex tails are; this is explained in Chapter 6. The ears are a little different. A short piece of 3X nylon is attached to a pin with tape. The pin is inserted into a piece of cardboard so the end of the nylon is touching the cardboard. A teardrop-shaped drop of liquid latex is injected onto the cardboard and around the tip of the nylon. The latex is allowed to cure, then latex is injected around the entire piece of nylon for durability.

2. The antennules are constructed next. Take two pieces of approximately ten-pound test mono and glue two tips of boars' bristles to each.

3. When the hook is inverted, tie in the eyes so they will be above the antennules. This fly will ride upside down, so if the hook were right-side up, the eyes would be below the antennules.

4. Tie in the antennules at the bend of the hook so they will be below the eye.

5. Tie in the ears to the side and slightly behind the eyes.

6. Tie in the raptorial legs below the antennules.

7. Tie in the antennae so they are below the antennules.

8. Tie in one or two pieces of flat lead strips on top of the hook more in back toward eye, so fly sits up when fished.

9. Tie in a bunch of golden cream Fish Fuzz behind the raptorial legs on the bottom of the hook shank behind the raptorial legs, leaving the back part—which is pointing toward the eye of the hook—very long, as it will form the abdomen and the tail.

10. Tie in a stiff cream cock hackle just behind the point where the carapace was tied in and wrap it toward the eye a short distance. Clip the top, which is on the bottom of the hook shank.

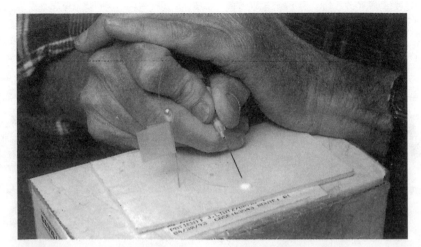

Tying procedure for Golden Mantis:
Constructing the ears (step 1).

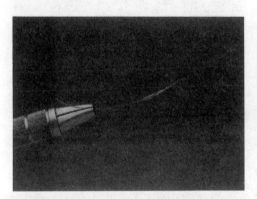

Constructing the antennulas (step 2).

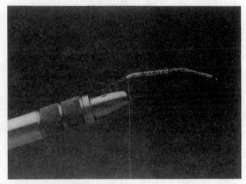

Tying in the eyes (step 3).

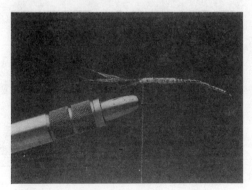

Tying in the antennulas (step 4).

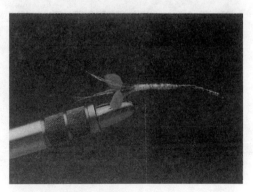

Tying in the ears (step 5).

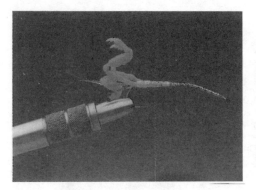

Tying the raptorial legs (steps 6–8).

Tying in the antennae and lead and the body (step 9).

Tying in the hackle and winding it (steps 10–11).

Step 12.

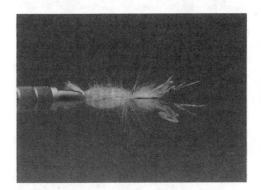

The colored fly (steps 13 and 14).

The finished fly from the front.

11. Tie in the short webby cree or light badger hackle and wrap it to the eye of the hook and clip short but not close to the hook.
12. Secure the Fish Fuzz laying back over the body to the hook just behind the eye to form the abdomen and tail fan.
13. Color the antennules, antennae, tails, raptorial legs, and abdominal segments with marking pens and/or liquid latex with acrylic paint.
14. Paint the eyes green with tiny black pupils.

An alternate method of coloring the ears, legs, abdominal segments, and tail is to use liquid latex mixed with liquid acrylic paint.

The antennules are yellow with orange segments, as are the ears, raptorial legs, and tails. The abdominal segments are yellow with an orange line in the middle of the yellow. When the latex is completely colored and cured, treat it with Armor-All to keep it supple.

An easier tie is very effective when rock mantis are present. This is almost as realistic as the more difficult tie because these thumpers hold their front claws tightly together, tucked in under their body rather than out, away from the body like the slashers. Merely substitute afterfeathers or maribou fiber on each side for the latex legs and tie in four simple antennae, rather than the complex ones on the first pattern. Substitute hackle tips for the ears, which can be attached with Super Glue. This pattern is deadly on flats close to reefs, and not only for bones; it takes permit also.

Tan Belizean mantis shrimp—carapace is tan grizzly hackle tips, and claws and front legs are light green afterfeathers.

Green Belizean mantis shrimp—carapace and claws are dark green afterfeathers.

Dark Belizean mantis shrimp—front legs and claws are blue-eared pheasant afterfeathers, carapace is blu-eared pheasant backfeathers.

Although mantis shrimp live in almost all types of water, I have found them most numerous on flats near reefs and on the slopes of the reef itself. Here they dart about in the shallow sand and rocky flats, and the populations are large. Snapping shrimp on the other hand seem much more common along the shoreline under rocks, shells, and other rubble. It seems only commonsensical to fish the corresponding imitations in their respective areas. The flies should be fished close to the bottom with a hopping retrieve and varying speeds. The mantis shrimp swims in short, quick sideways bursts. The imitations should be fished so they swim like the naturals; they should not be retrieved straight back in the traditional bonefish manner. The sideways motion can be achieved by moving the rod tip from side to side on alternate strips.

CHAPTER SIXTEEN

Tying Sea Urchins

This pattern very closely imitates sea urchins, yet it is very simple and easy to tie. Sea urchins are abundant and obvious inhabitants of lagoons and turtle grass beds. They are slow-moving grazers, exist in every shallow water niche, and are fed upon by bonefish and permit.

The most common species in turtle grass beds is the variable or green sea urchin (*Lytechinus variegatus*), and the sea egg (*Tripneustes ventricous*). The species I am most familiar with is the red rock urchin (*Echinometra lucumter*), which I have encountered in the Yucatan. Permit regularly come into the lagoon at Casa Blanca Bonefish Lodge to feed on this species. Sea urchins consist of a main body called a test, which has a variable shape. Spines protrude from this test, and that is the simple animal we are imitating.

Red Rock Urchin

Color Spines are red, reddish black, or reddish brown, but there is almost always some red at the base of the spines, which are ¾- to 1-inch long. The test is mainly black and is the same diameter as the length of the spines.

Habitat Rocky shores just below the water's surface.

Range Florida, Texas, Mexico, Bermuda, Jamaica, the West Indies, to Brazil.

Variable or Green Sea Urchin

Color Spines, long, greenish white, white, or white with purple tips. The test is light green, or poda white and white to 3 inches long. Spines are ½-inch long.

Habitat Turtle grass beds.

Range Florida, the Bahamas, and West Indies; North Carolina.

Sea Egg

Color White, ½-inch long spines, and black, purple, or brown test.

Habitat Turtle grass beds.

Range Florida, Bermuda, Bahamas, West Indies, Jamaica, Trinidad, to Brazil.

Many other species exist worldwide with diverse shapes, sizes, and colors, so, as always, it is advisable to capture specimens where you are fishing. Urchins should be fished on the bottom with a very slow, steady retrieve.

Red Rock Urchin—Materials

HOOK	Mustad AC 34068 #4, #6
THREAD	White monochord 3/0
TEST	Flattened splitshot covered with liquid latex mixed with red acrylic paint
SPINES	Black or red-brown deer hair or silly legs

Tying Instructions

1. Spin deer hair on hook and clip short on the top of the hook.
2. Flatten a splitshot with a hammer and cement to top of hook with five-minute epoxy.
3. Paint the splitshot with liquid latex mixed with a little red acrylic paint, working some into the base of the deer-hair spines for strength.
4. Repaint with black latex, leaving some red showing on the top.

Tying in the first clump of deer hair.

All the hair tied in and trimmed.

Step 2.

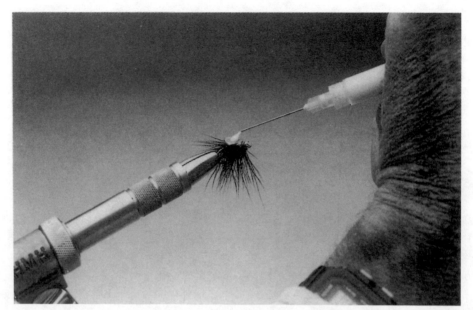

Step 3.

The finished fly (step 4).

CHAPTER SEVENTEEN

Tying the Shrimpys

Two Impressionistic Ties for All Shrimp Species

These are two simple but effective patterns that are impressionistic for all the various types of shrimp. They are composed of materials that undulate in the water, producing an enticing swimming action as they are retrieved. There are two basic patterns; one I call the Hair Shrimpy and the other I call the Feather Shrimpy. These two pattern types, when dressed in various sizes and colors, will successfully simulate any shrimp species, from the large, mature swimming shrimp all the way down to tiny grass and shore shrimp.

The many species of the shrimp families come in about any color combination you can think of, but with the six variations I will list, you can deceive most gamefish in most situations.

	Feather Version	Hair Version
1. Tan Shrimpy		
BODY	Tan mohair	Tan mohair
HACKLE	Cree and grizzly mixed	None
WINGS	One cree, grizzly, and honey badger on each side	White sheep fleece under tan sheep fleece

EYES	Burnt mono	Same
ANTENNAE	Boars' bristles and Crystalflash	Same

2. Pink Shrimpy

BODY	Pink mohair	Same
HACKLE	Pink and grizzly	None
WINGS	One pink, grizzly, and honey badger on each side	Pink sheep fleece over white sheep fleece
EYES	Burnt mono	Same
ANTENNAE	Boars' bristles and Crystalflash	Same

3. Cream Shrimpy

BODY	Cream mohair	Same
HACKLE	Cree and honey badger	None
WINGS	One light grizzly, honey badger, and cree on each side	Cream and tan sheep fleece
EYES	Burnt mono	Same
ANTENNAE	Boars' bristles and Crystalflash	Same

4. Green Shrimpy

BODY	Green mohair	Same
HACKLE	Olive and grizzly	None
WINGS	One grizzly, green cree, and olive badger on each side	Green sheep fleece over cream sheep fleece
EYES	Burnt mono	Same
ANTENNAE	Boars' bristles and Crystalflash	Same

5. Yellow Shrimpy

BODY	Yellow mohair	Same
HACKLE	Yellow grizzly and cree	None
WINGS	One yellow badger, grizzly, and honey badger on each side	Yellow mohair over cream mohair

EYES	Burnt mono	Same
ANTENNAE	Boars' bristles and Crystalflash	Same

6. Brown Shrimpy

BODY	Brown mohair	Same
HACKLE	Brown and grizzly	None
WINGS	One grizzly, brown, and honey badger on each side	Brown mohair over cream mohair
EYES	Burnt mono	Same
ANTENNAE	Boars' bristles and Crystalflash	Same

These patterns can be tied weighted or unweighted, and to ride with the hook up or down, depending on conditions. I usually use #2 to #8 hooks for bonefish; #2 to #4 for baby tarpon, snook, and redfish; and #2/0 to #1 for giant tarpon.

Feather Shrimpy

Tying Instructions

1. Tie in eyes at hook bend.
2. Tie in a piece of flat lead if you want a fast-sinking fly.
3. Tie in the antennae.
4. Tie in a little ball of mohair yarn just behind the eyes.
5. Tie in three hackles of the desired shades on each side of the ball of yarn.
6. Wind the hackle behind the wings.

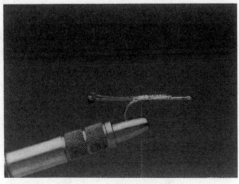

Step 1.

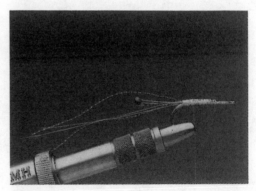

Steps 2 and 3.

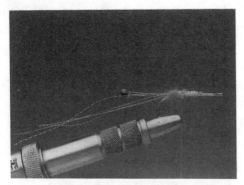

Step 4.

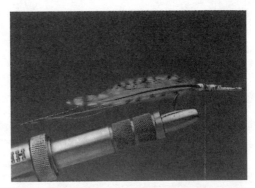

Step 5.

Step 6.

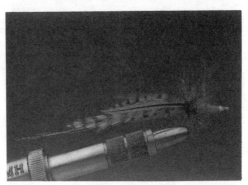

Steps 7 and 8.

7. Tie in the mohair yarn and wrap to the eye of the hook. It is important to brush the little fibers of the mohair out so you do not trap them under as you wrap the yarn.
8. Tie off head and cement with five-minute epoxy.

Hair Shrimpy
Tying Instructions

1. Tie in the eyes at the hook bend.
2. Tie in lead if desired.
3. Tie in the antennae.
4. Tie in a bunch of sheep fleece at the hook bend so it goes back over the eyes and a little beyond.
5. Tie in a strip of mohair yarn and wrap to the eye of the hook.

6. Tie in a bunch of sheep fleece so it goes back to the bend of the hook and a little goes forward for the tail.
7. Wrap the tail down, tie off, and cement the head with five-minute epoxy.

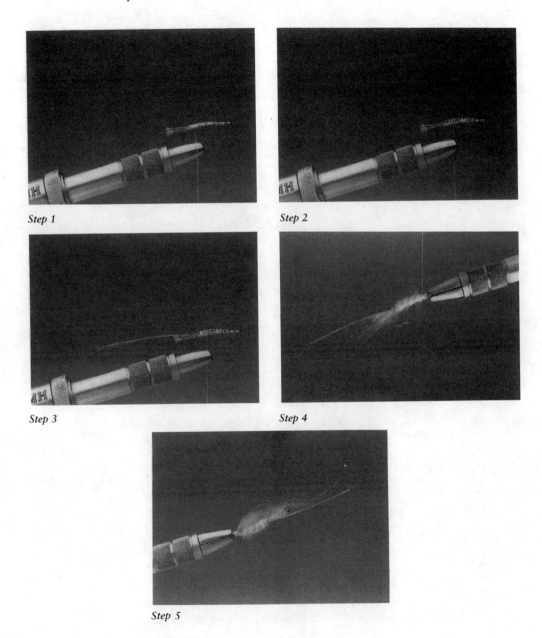

Step 1

Step 2

Step 3

Step 4

Step 5

CHAPTER EIGHTEEN

Constructing an Attachable Weed Guard

Weed guards can at times be a necessary evil. I don't like to use them if I don't really need to, but sometimes in heavy grass or coral they are unavoidable. I also do not like to tie my flies with them when I only occasionally use them, and I do not want to keep two sets of flies, one with weed guards and one without. I solved this dilemma by constructing a set of attachable weed guards that slip over the eye of the hook easily and quickly. Now when I find a compelling need to use one, I just attach it to the fly as I am fishing.

Weed-guarded fly swimming through the weeds.

The weed guards are made of wire and orthodontic acrylic resin. The flat eye of the hook holds them in place and keeps them from twisting. I need to have several sizes to match the hook sizes I am fishing with. They are easy to make and much more convenient to carry than a separate set of flies with built-in weed guards.

Materials

Wire from a hobby shop, orthodontic resin (liquid and powder mixture from a dentist), polyvinylsiloxane impression material from a dentist, candle wax

Construction Instructions

1. Take a bare hook, place it in the vise, and wrap an eye with fly-tying thread.
2. Tie on a piece of leader material to the hook eye using the same type of knot you use when fishing. I use an improved clinch knot, but any knot except a loop knot will work as long as it is not too bulky.
3. Place five-minute epoxy over the eye of the fly, the eye of the hook, and the knot in the leader material in such a way as to block out all the undercuts.
4. Take some wax, melt it, and place it on the parts you have epoxied to form a smooth, bullet-shaped head.
5. Take a small plastic cup and cut it as illustrated.

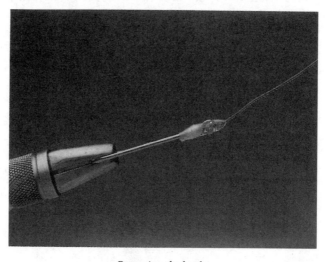

Preparing the hook.

The mold with the liquid plastic and wire in place.

6. Pierce the cup at one end and stick the leader material attached to the hook through the hole.
7. Mix the impression material and place it around the hook and the bottom half of waxed head. The impression material will harden in about five minutes and will form a permanent rubbery mold.
8. Remove the hook from the mold and remove the wax from the hook eye with boiling water.
9. Replace the hook in the mold and mix the liquid and powdered resin into a thick, soupy liquid, and place it in the mold around the hook eye and the knot in the leader.
10. Take a piece of wire and bend it as illustrated and place it on the eye of the hook.
11. Place a few drops of liquid resin over the hook eye and the bend in the hook.
12. Allow the resin to harden; this takes about ten minutes, but hot water will accelerate the process.
13. Remove the hook from the mold and remove the weed guard from the hook. If the weed guard is not smooth or has voids, you can mix more liquid plastic and fill in the voids.
14. Smooth the plastic with an acrylic burr, then with a cloth-polishing wheel and watered flour pumice. These can be obtained in hobby shops or from your dentist. You could smooth it with sandpaper, but the dental way is the easiest.

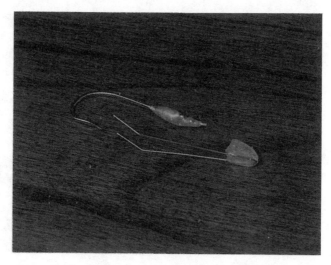

The finished weed guard with prepared hook.

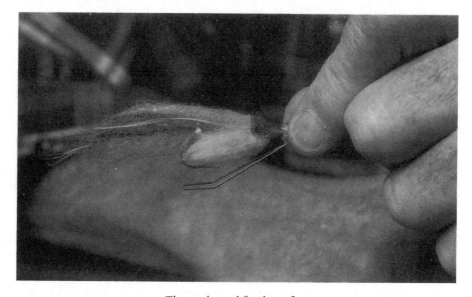

The weed guard fitted to a fly.

You now have an attachable weed guard and a permanent mold to make more, as necessary.

An Easy Weed Guard for Flies Already Tied

If you do not want to go to the trouble of constructing a detachable weed guard—which is admittedly a lot easier to construct if you happen to be a dentist and are used to working with these materials—a very practical alternative is the mono loop. This can be added to a fly after it has been tied, as the necessity arises. You will need a tying vise and some thread. A length of mono is burned on both ends to form little balls. This is then tied at the eye of the hook with a figure-eight wrap. The loop hangs straight down and should be just a hair short of the point when the loop is bent back. It looks strange, and you wouldn't think it would be effective, but it is one of the most efficient weed guards I have ever used.

CHAPTER NINETEEN

Tactics for Selective Fresh and Saltwater Gamefish Using Close Imitations

Saltwater gamefish, like freshwater fish, become extremely selective when feeding on prey that is swarming in huge numbers. These gamefish feed much like trout that are feeding on a spinner fall of Tricos. That is to say, they almost always take more than one creature at a time, usually many more. Like trout, they will consume surprisingly small food forms, considering the size of the fish, and when they do, they know exactly what they want. The reason they do consume this tiny forage is the fact that the forage occur in very large numbers and many can be taken in one gulp. If gamefish could not swallow ten or twenty in one pass, they would not feed on the minute forms, since it would take more energy to capture the food than they would gain.

One of the exceptions to this kind of feeding is the migration of swimming shrimps from the inside bays where they mature to the open gulf where they spend their adult lives. During this migration, millions of young adult shrimp drift and swim through the passes on strong outgoing tides, almost always at night under a full or new moon. The migration is heaviest from late spring to late fall, but occurs

Swarm of baitfish.

117

Migrating swimming shrimp.

all year long in lesser numbers. These shrimp are large enough (from two to three inches long) and packed with a great amount of nutrition so the predators will take them one at a time. Nevertheless, gamefish become ultraselective during the migrations—close imitations are necessary.

The other exception is the inward migration of juvenile swimming crabs called "pass crabs." These are hatched in the open gulf and move to the inside waterways to mature. They are also large enough (three-quarters to an inch wide) so the gamefish will feed on them individually, but again a close imitation is required.

Fishing the shrimp and crab migrations is easy, providing you have a realistic imitation, as they are taken one at a time. However, fishing to gamesters feeding on schools of swarming baitfish requires a more specialized technique. Since they are taking many individuals at a time and they see so many of them, not only must the imitation be a good one but it must be fished among the swarm of naturals. If it is not in the swarm, it will almost certainly not be taken, as the fish require more than one natural in a gulp. Not only do you need a close imitation to fool the gamefish, but a close imitation is also necessary to fool the baitfish. If your fly is too large, it will frighten the school of baitfish, and they will shy away from it. Your fly will no longer be in the swarm.

There are two types of fishing to these swarms, daytime and nighttime. Nighttime angling is the simplest, as the baitfish are attracted to lights under bridges, docks, and pilings. If your imitation doesn't frighten them, it's easy to keep it in the school because they will not leave the lights. The naturals swim

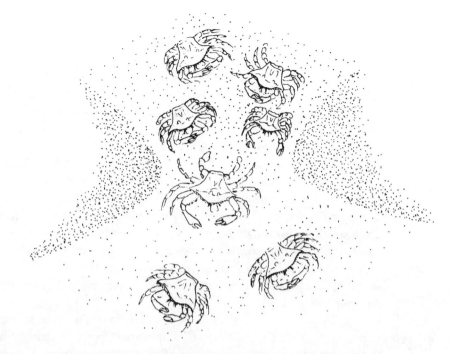

Young blue swimming crabs migrating in through a pass.

Richards in a boat, fishing to a lighted dock with fish feeding under it.

in a short, jerky motion and a realistic fly manipulated to swim in the same manner is deadly.

Daylight fishing to swarms of baitfish is very different and much more difficult. In fact, occasionally it is almost impossible. Here again, the fly must swim with the school, but the school is moving. When you are imitating relatively large baitfish such as thread herring, finger mullet, or Spanish sardines, you are dealing with a swarm that is large in area. It's difficult but not impossible to intercept the prey; cast into it and keep in contact with it with a boat using an electric motor. Keep an eye on the birds, since they will help you find the school and keep in contact with it. Onshore bait such as Atlantic silversides and sand eels, which are found in large numbers around Martha's Vineyard, Cape Cod, and Long Island Sound, are fed upon by striped bass and bluefish. These small, slim prey stay close to the beach and the cuts, so it is much easier to keep your fly in the school.

Very small bait is more difficult to fish to. It is amazing, at least to me, how tiny some naturals are that fall prey to much larger fish. Previously, I had seen snook up to ten pounds, jack cravelle up to six pounds, and tarpon up to fifteen pounds take quarter-inch glass minnows and bay anchovies under the lights. That seemed strange at first, but as long as I used a reasonable imitation in the

A lagoon on the Blackwater River with tarpon feeding on baby sailfin mollies.

correct size and manipulated it in short, quick jerks, I had no trouble hooking fish. This winter, I was astounded when I discovered small pods of five- to fifteen-pound tarpon five miles up Florida's Blackwater River feeding on schools of baby sailfin mollys. These mollys were only ⅜-inch long, but the tarpon were busting the schools all morning long. The schools were two to three feet in diameter, moving slowly on the surface and creating "nervous" water. I could watch the schools move, but when I cast in the middle of one, the fish scattered. If I cast a ⅜-inch imitation a few feet to the side and worked it into the school, the naturals would swim along with it, at least for a while. I have had some success creating my own school of baby sailfins by tying five or six artificials in tandem on the leader, but even then it was much more effective if my school swam with, or at least beside, the real school. This was difficult fishing to say the least, and actually landing the tarpon when I did hook one was only luck considering the light tippets necessary to tie on such small imitations and the abrasive mouths of the tarpon.

Smaller gamefish such as five- to ten-pound snook will take some of the larger schooling baitfish one at a time. Thread herring and scaled and Spanish sardines can reach fairly large size, three to four inches and even larger. These are big enough and nutritious enough to be attacked singly. However, very large gamefish will crash the schools, taking even big forage many individuals at a time. Last summer, I was anchored under the 951 Bridge, which connects Marco Island to the Tamiami Trail. It was two o'clock in the morning, a full moon was shining, and a strong incoming tide was ripping in at about six knots. Some very nice snook were taking three-inch thread herring. I had a good imitation and had no trouble hooking over twenty fish up to ten pounds

Big tarpon busting up through a school of baitfish.

because the snook were taking the herring singly. As the tide reached peak flow at about three-thirty, four large tarpon began crashing the school. The largest was about eighty pounds. His attacks on the school of herring created a hellacious racket, which was repeated exactly every three minutes. There was no point in casting to this fish in between the three-minute intervals because he immediately returned to the bottom to digest his meal. When he became ready to feed again, he would rise and crash through the school, roll on the surface, and return to the bottom.

My strategy in this situation was to time the interval between his feeding rushes and attempt to have my fly in the swarm of baitfish at the right time in the right place. Unfortunately, the big tarpon never rose in exactly the same place. He would move to the right or left without seeming reason, although he must have had a reason that I never did figure out. I never got that fish to take my imitation, but I think I fished him the only way possible. I did, at the later stages of the tide, try some wildly different patterns such as large ladyfish and mullet, but that didn't work either. The difficulty in this situation was the right artificial had to be in the exact area of the school of baitfish the tarpon had decided to attack next and only he knew where that was.

Bottom feeders (bonefish, permit, and redfish) also become selective. The condition necessary for this selectivity appears to be an extreme density of a single prey species on a flat or bay. These fish take the prey singly, which makes it much easier to get strikes. All that is needed is a good imitation that can be manipulated to swim and crawl like the natural.

Certain species of prey do appear in great density in the areas I fish for bones, permit, and redfish. On the Gulf Coast of Florida, the flats and bays

Redfish tailing for crabs around oyster shells.

Nervous water—a school of bonefish on the move.

have mostly mangrove borders, the roots of which harbor oysters. The oyster shells in turn harbor literally millions of small mud crabs and tiny porcelain crabs. These crabs appear to be the preferred food of the local redfish and sheepshead populations. I have observed guides from Port of the Islands cleaning redfish, and all were stuffed with the small crabs and nothing else. My imitations are designed to dive in the headfirst position, but crawl sideways; this mimics the naturals I have observed. I fish them crawling slowly on the bottom, occasionally adding a few quick strips.

Bonefish and permit in the Florida Keys, the Bahamas, Ascension Bay in the Yucatan, and Turneffe Reed in Belize have also become selective to crabs. Where they are mangrove islands and bays, the same mud and porcelain crabs are abundant; however, out on the open flats, green reef crabs are not only numerous but swarming, and the gamefish come to gorge on these small crustaceans during the flooding tide. The artificials are fished the same as for redfish. This is another instance of very small imitations taking very large fish.

Bonefish in the Bahamas and the Florida Keys often are selective to banded snapping shrimp. I have collected these shrimp in the Berry Islands, Bahamas, when I easily captured over a hundred in ten minutes by turning over shells along the shore at low tide. A. J. McClane stated that he found forty banded snapping shrimp in one bonefish and that this species was the most-eaten prey in the Florida Keys and the Bahamas.

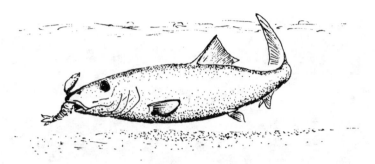

Bonefish eating banded snapping shrimp.

Snook coming out of the water after a jumping shrimp.

Bonefish for some reason become selective to shrimp-shaped flies tied in the color pink and pink-and-white. I am not sure why this is, but I have had experiences in the Yucatan and the Bahamas where pink Shrimpys outfished everything else twenty to one. There are a number of species of pink-and-red shrimp in this range and also some gobies and blennies have this coloration, but I do not know exactly which creature causes this color preference. I do know never to try to fish these locations without some pink Shrimpys in sizes #2 through #8.

When fishing for bonefish, snapping shrimp and swimming shrimp are usually fished on the bottom with varying retrieves. The artificials are designed to face their attacker as the naturals do. The swimming shrimp imitation that I use during the shrimp migrations when fishing for snook and tarpon is worked just under the surface with a slow retrieve. It can also be drifted, so it appears to be swimming with the tidal flow in the direction of the flow. I give it a few fast strips when I think a fish is after it and even make it jump out of the water like the naturals do when they are being chased by a predator. This often arouses the competitive instinct in gamefish and they will chase the fly while it is in the air. That kind of take is spectacular.

Shark and barracuda on the flats do not seem to be selective as I think of selectivity, however some imitations outperform most others by a wide margin. One such imitation is the frill-finned goby. Gobies are a comparatively slow-swimming family of fishes that resemble freshwater sculpin. They are readily taken by sharks, barracuda, and large bonefish probably because, once spotted, they are easy to catch. I have had my entire collection of gobies destroyed by sharks while I was fishing for bonefish because I was not using a wire leader. Sharks and barracuda also show a decided liking for juvenile bonefish when they can trap them. I have enjoyed a lot of success with an imitation of these fish that I try to manipulate so they appear crippled.

Everyone acknowledges that freshwater gamefish become selective when a prey species becomes dense, but most only think of mayflies, caddis flies, midges, or other insect forms. The appearance of soft-shelled crayfish along the shore, and in the shallows of a river after the molt, creates a selective event and also a fabulous fishing opportunity. After the "kicking out" process, a river's shallows can become carpeted with these miniature lobsters. Bass and

Barracuda after a bonefish.

Summer steelhead after a soft-shelled crab.

Big brown trout after a small brook trout.

trout seem to crave these creatures as much as people crave Maine lobsters. Fish go on a feeding binge after a molt, and a good imitation of a soft-shell, fished on the bottom or drifting in the current, will reward the angler with fish of a size unlikely to be taken during an insect emergence.

Another event which is not usually exploited by the freshwater fly fisherman, but which can produce really huge brown trout, is not an insect emergence, but is created by that emergence. When a hatch takes place, all the small trout come out from hiding and begin feeding on the insects. They now lose much of their usual caution. The real lunker trout roam the riffles looking for a sizable meal that small insects do not provide but small trout do. Big browns really like to eat small and not-so-small brook trout when the brookies are distracted by the hatch.

Smelt runs—which occur in the early spring with the rainbow smelt running out of lakes into streams to spawn—find large freshwater gamefish such as landlocked salmon and big browns cruising the beaches off the mouths of the streams. They provide spectacular fly rodding when opening day has not arrived on most trout waters, and will smash a good imitation fished on a floating line with fast strips.

Whether I am fishing fresh or salt, I want a pattern that closely resembles the prey my quarry is eating. After all, the very best chance of hooking many fish, or a trophy fish, is when they are feeding heavily. The very reason they are feeding heavily is that there is a lot of something to feed on and that is the precise time when gamefish are the most selective! When the best fishing occurs, I want the best pattern I can tie of whatever prey is swarming, whether it be mayflies or crayfish for trout and bass, sardines for tarpon, or snapping shrimp for bonefish.

Coda

The study of forage species and designing patterns to imitate them has given me much pleasure over the years. It is especially rewarding when the patterns prove productive. Much work remains to be done in the area, especially in salt and brackish water, because so little is known about many of the food gamefish eat. I can anticipate years of enjoyment in the future. I have found that if I go on a vacation to an exotic destination and catch (or not catch) a lot of fish, I have fun and I enjoy myself, but when I am back home it is over. When I take the little time necessary to collect minnows, crabs, shrimp, etc., that live in that exotic location, and get some pictures of them, my enjoyment is not ended when the fishing trip is over. I can now look forward to getting the film developed, studying the results, and designing new and better patterns than I originally had. I can then look forward to returning and hopefully having better success than I had the first time.

Quite often I get a shot that is of great significance, at least to me. For instance, upon returning from the Berry Islands last year, I discovered I had a shot of banded snapping shrimp. When I studied this species, I found that A. J. McClane had written that bonefish in the Bahamas and the Florida Keys eat more of this shrimp by numbers than any other forage. As far as I know, those shots I took are the only pictures in existence of banded snapping shrimp. To me, and presumably to other bonefishermen, these shots are of great significance, as I doubt I could ever have tied a reasonable imitation without the picture.

On my last trip to the 10,000 Islands in December, I found an inside area in the backcountry where baby tarpon and large snook were riding out the cold weather and feeding on sail-finned mollies. These are the same species that home fish fanciers keep in freshwater aquariums, although they like brackish water better. If I hadn't taken the time to use the dip net, I would never have discovered a very useful winter-time pattern.

On that same trip, I took a few minutes to walk on an oyster bar at low tide and found thousands of pea crabs, a little-known species that redfish gorge on in shallow water. Almost every trip I learn something new so when I return home I can keep myself entertained until the next trip. If there were nothing new to learn, fly fishing would soon become boring, for catching fish alone is not enough. The one thing that makes fly fishing such a great sport is that there is always something new to learn, so it is always interesting. I sincerely hope this book will help make the sport more enjoyable for you.

Bibliography

Science

Boschung, Jr., Herbert T. et al. *The Audubon Society Field Guide to North American Fishes, Whales, and Dolphins*. New York: Alfred A. Knopf, 1983.

Eschmeyer, William N. *A Field Guide to Pacific Coast Fishes of North America*. Boston: Houghton Mifflin, 1983.

Hoese, H. Dickson, and Richard H. Moore. *Fishes of the Gulf of Mexico*. College Station, TX: Texas A&M University Press, 1977.

Manning, Raymond B. *Stomatopod Crustacea of the Western Atlantic*. Miami: University of Miami Press, 1969.

Kaplan, Eugene H. *A Field Guide to Coral Reefs*. Boston: Houghton Mifflin, 1982.

Kaplan, Eugene H. *A Field Guide to Southeastern and Caribbean Seashores*. Boston: Houghton Mifflin, 1988.

Meinkoth, Norman A. *The Audubon Society Field Guide to North American Sea Shore Creatures*. New York: Alfred A. Knopf, 1981.

Page, Lawrence M., and Brooks M. Burr. *A Field Guide to Fresh Water Fishes*. Boston: Houghton Mifflin, 1991.

Robins, C. Richard. *A Field Guide to Atlantic Coast Fishes of North America*. Boston: Houghton Mifflin, 1986.

Walls, Jerry G. *Encyclopedia of Marine Invertebrates*. Neptune, NJ: T. F. H. Publications, 1982.

Williams, Auston B. *Shrimps, Lobsters and Crabs of the Atlantic Coast of the Eastern United States, Maine to Florida*. Washington, DC: Smithsonian Institution Press, 1984.

Fishing

Allen, Farrow, and Dick Stewart. *Flies for Saltwater*. Mounton Pond Publishing, 1992.

Bauer, Erwin A. *The Saltwater Fisherman's Bible*. New York: Doubleday, 1991.

Brown, Dick. *Fly Fishing for Bonefish*. New York: Lyons & Burford, 1993.

McClane, A. J., and Keith Gardner. *Game Fish of North America*. Bonanza Books, 1984.

Kreh, Lefty. *Salt Water Fly Patterns*. Maral, Inc., 1991.

Kreh, Lefty, and Mark Sosin. *Fishing the Flats*. New York: Lyons & Burford, 1983.

Sargent, Frank. *The Snook Book*. Lakeland, FL: Larsen's Outdoor Publishing, 1991.

———. *The Redfish Book*. Lakeland, FL: Larsen's Outdoor Publishing, 1991.

———. *The Tarpon Book*. Lakeland, FL: Larsen's Outdoor Publishing, 1991.

———. *The Trout Book*. Lakeland, FL: Larsen's Outdoor Publishing, 1991.

Tabory, Lou. *Inshore Fly Fishing*. New York: Lyons & Burford, 1992.

Wentink, Frank. *Saltwater Fly Tying*. New York: Lyons & Burford, 1991.

Index